Inline!

Inline!

A *Manual* for Beginning to Intermediate Inline *Skating*

william nealy

 Menasha Ridge Press
BIRMINGHAM, AL

Library of Congress
Cataloging-in-Publication Data

Nealy, William, 1953–2001
    Inline! : a manual of inter-
mediate to advanced technique
/ by William nealy. — 1st ed.
        p.   cm.
    ISBN 0-89732-274-6
    1. In-line skating. 2. In-line
skating—Humor. I. Title.
GV859.73.N43 1998
796.21—dc21
                    98-17921
                        CIP

Printed in
   the United States of America

Published by
   Menasha Ridge Press
Distributed by
   the Globe Pequot Press

First Edition, Second Printing 2003

Book design and illustrations by
   William Nealy
Cover design by
   Grant M. Tatum

Menasha Ridge Press
P.O. Box 43673
Birmingham, AL 35243
www.menasharidge.com

Acknowledgments

First, thanks to my love and editor-in-chief Holly "Dr. H." Wallace who edited and assembled this book, kept me together and put up with a couple years of blading craziness.

Thanks to Durham North Carolina's "Wigs On Wheels", who taught me how to skate: Simone DeButt, Steph ("Stella") & Jeff Hartman, David Dwyer, Shaub Dunkley, and Van Wilson. Also my support and advice team: Barb & Stan Martinkosky, Tessa Perrien, Carl & Darcy Siebert, Tom Stephenson, my mom, and my little skating buddies (read "lab mice") Basie Settle and Henry Wallace who are surviving nephewdom splendidly!

Special thanks to technical editor Holly Kemp and my dudes at Menasha: Bud Zehmer and Mike Jones. Finally, thanks to Mary Charles Painter, who taught me to draw, Betty Foley Caldwell, who taught me how to write, and Larry Hewitt, who gave me the idea for this book a few years ago.

V

To Edgar Hitchcock
a.k.a. "Ocho Rios"
1953 - 1994
Sportsman, Renaissance Man, Pirate
I miss you, my brother...

Table of Contents

Act One, Scene One : My regular orthopedic surgeon's office, Fall-1996

Bill... you're middle-aged, asthmatic, your knees are blown, your lumbar spine is degenerated and osteoarthritic, your right rotator cuff is hamburger, and one more head injury and you'll be working at the sheltered workshop. NO more skiing, canoeing, backpacking, kayaking, mountain biking, rock climbing, snow or skateboarding and anything resembling a contact sport! Got that!?

"William", not Bill! Jeez, I've only been your patient for nine years...

He didn't say a damn thing about INLINE SKATING! Heh heh heh...

The only kind of
rail I'll grind...

Inline skating is like skiing black dia-
monds, _being_ a ferrari (!), and, sometimes,
robbing a bank! Ordinary pavement becomes sets
of waves, turning our "civilization" into **SURF!**
It's intoxicating and addictive. In short, inline
skating is way too much fun and probably
should be illegal (or regulated by the F.D.A. at least).

This book depicts just **one** of the **many paths** to
Inline Skating Nirvana. It's a fairly accurate record
of the joy I've experienced, the insights I've had
and the **many mistakes** I've made while learning
to be a **competant recreational street skater.**
My "crash and burn" learning philosophy may not
be for you _but_ you can learn lots from my mistakes as well as my successes. Perhaps you'll discover
a shortcut on the road to becoming a better skater.

I've attempted to arrange all techniques,
skills, & definitions in "**learning order**" (**easy →
difficult → most difficult**) so for maximum under-
standing of the really complicated skills read
the whole chapter **first**, then concentrate on
individual moves. The emphasis here is on movement "**flow**" and gradually **building up moves**, not working backwards from snapshots of the end result
of **polished** moves. Go slow, remember to have fun and
above all, be kind to your student (yourself).

I've intentionally omitted material on racing,
dance, vert, five-wheeling, roller hockey, grinding,
rail-sliding, stretching and diet. The other books have
covered the subjects at length. My focus is on the
steps to becoming an advanced-intermediate
skater, the prerequisite to all the activities above.
I've also tried to avoid discussion of specific products and technology for two reasons: ① Products
and technology change a couple times a

1

year therefore rendering meaningful discussion instantly **obsolete**, and ② Until you've accumulated significant miles actually **skating**, any decision you make as to what skates or accessories you should purchase is in reality an **uneducated** guess. Although I advocate a **self-teaching** approach to skating, if you have the resources by all means **take lessons** from qualified instructors, go to **skate camp**, join a **skating club**! You'll avoid some road rash and, the more you skate with other **competant skaters**, the better skater you'll **become**.

Relax dude... everybody looks incredibly silly to somebody!

gasp!

umph!

awk!

oof!

INline Skating is an inherently dangerous sport! You will Notice that this book generally takes a very conservative approach to all forms of recreational skating activities. For beginners, helmets and excessive pads are mandatory! I've depicted the occasional helmetless and unar- mored skater for artistic and instructional purposes; body armor conceals subtle body movement and I get tired of drawing humAN armadillos. You choose your style (conservative vs. extreme) and your skating environment ["safe"(no hills, no cars) vs."extreme" (traffic, drops, high speed)] therefore you are ultimately responsible for the consequences of your choices! ["Bad Boy Rule #1] No one can make you be a safe skater but you!

The next few pages ("Introduction") consist of diagrams and terminology meant to acquaint you with my technical vocabulary and help you interpret the illustrations you'll see later in the book. On first reading, these terms and diagrams will probably make little or no sense to you but (I hope) the technical stuff will become clear to you as you go along. As I've suggested, read this book in skill sections to get a feel for the flow and evolution of skills. Worry about the technical details (foot weighting, use of edges, leg tilt, vectors, etc.) after your skills and experience increase during the learning process.

4

Introduction

Key To Illustrations

To avoid ridiculously excessive technospeak, I've tried to depict in each drawing enough information for you to understand what's going on in some pretty complex movement sequences...

Symbols

left skate

right skate

50/50 weight distribution

weight shift

①,②,③ main move sequence

③ⓐ,ⓑ move components

power stroke - length & direction

unweighted skate shift (scissor)

skate tilt

Skater Tilt (lean) shown by shadow

Example: Crossover Turn

Torso twist ①

②

Original Vector

Step over

Cross-under stroke

Scissor forward wt. 50/50

③ⓐ

New Vector

Example -

Skate Angle slightly exaggerated ②

① micro-vector

Heel-Toe 180° Spin

① "Inside" foot (left) weighted 80% heelward, "outside" foot weighted 20% toeward...

② Spin 180°, wt. shift to rt. foot to finish

Speed Lines...

Very Fast

Slow

flakey

5

Introduction, cont'd...

Body Configuration...

lycra

Tucked (closed stance)

Untucked (open)

Way Open "Air Brakes"

Antilycra

Turn

Inside / Outside

Wide Spin (epicycle)

Inside / Outside

Turns, spins and arcs...

Inside / Outside

Arc

Tight Spin "outside"

Body Armor

Pad use may vary according to your style and skating environment...

helmet →

elbow pad

faceguard

Thick, baggy clothes

hard elbow pads

massive wrist guard/glove

hockey girdle

wrist guard

"Extreme" kneepad

shinguard

minor kneepad

"beach armor"

All About Rocker...

Unrockered - All wheels on ground, best recreational configuration. medium maneuverability, great cruising.

Rockered - 2 to 3 wheels on the ground; quick turns and spins

Anti-Rocker - center wheels off the ground... a two-wheeler. Good for grinds, rail slides...

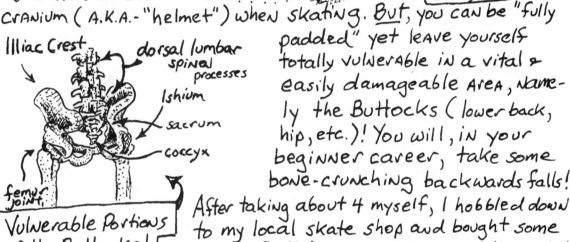

Hockey Pads — front view

It's normal and routine for the beginner to wear pads on the shins, elbows, wrists, knees as well as an exo-cranium (A.K.A.-"helmet") when skating. But, you can be "fully padded" yet leave yourself totally vulnerable in a vital & easily damageable area, namely the Buttocks (lower back, hip, etc.)! You will, in your beginner career, take some bone-crunching backwards falls!

Illiac Crest

dorsal lumbar spinal processes

Ishium

sacrum

coccyx

femur joint.

Vulnerable Portions of the Buttockal Region

After taking about 4 myself, I hobbled down to my local skate shop and bought some serious **Butt Armor**... hockey goalie pads/pants ornamented with lots of big plastic plates and generous 1" foam padding. Admittedly, I looked like a ninja turtle dressed-out and people made fun but with the added padding I was able to avoid "buttfall phobia" and stay on the learning curve without "post-traumatic buttfall syndrome" psychotherapy. Later I acquired some "Crashpads™"* that work great, and are concealable so nobody thinks you're an extreme weenie. I highly recommend buttfall abstinence whenever possible but just in case, carry some serious protection... the "Butt Helmet!"

Q: Why do fashionable skater dudes wear baggy clothes? A: To hide their body armor!

Crash Pads

---

* unpaid product endorsement

Introduction, cont'd...

Skate Anatomy

upper boot
cuff
tongue
mid-foot
lower boot
Toe
heel
wheel "frame"
brake
wheels

midline (center)
cutaway
ball of foot
toe
Inside edge
edge of foot (outside edge)
center edge

Functional Anatomy

Foot weight/pressure center of boot

Heel Tilt
Toe Tilt

Leg Torque
Leg Tilt

"outside"
"inside"
Foot Weighting
Ankle Cant ("break")
Toe pressure

How Inline Skates Work

Weighting the toes & applying leg torque Cause your skates to pivot up to 180° on your toes

① Leg Torque

Shin pressure on tongues!

② Follow through, skates follow twisting leg 180°

Toe Pivot Spin 180°

Inside toe pressure and leg tilt Cause your skate to turn "inside"

Leg Tilt
Ankle Cant

Ankle "break" to inside increases edge friction

Leg Tilt
Ankle cant

more friction, less speed !

Introduction, cont'd...

In physics, "vectors" are straight lines. I curve my cartoon vectors to depict the skater's complex **path** thru space & time. Spins, pivots, strokes, etc. occur in the vector. Turns, stepovers and jumps create new vectors.

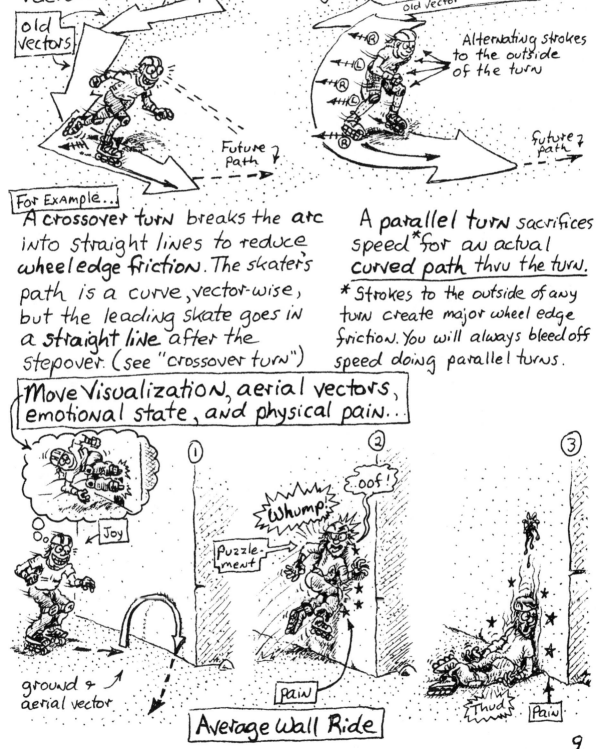

old vectors

old vector

Alternating strokes to the outside of the turn

Future Path

future path

For Example..

A **crossover turn** breaks the arc into straight lines to reduce wheel edge friction. The skater's path is a curve, vector-wise, but the leading skate goes in a **straight line** after the stepover. (see "crossover turn")

A **parallel turn** sacrifices speed* for an actual curved path thru the turn.

* Strokes to the outside of any turn create major wheel edge friction. You will always bleed off speed doing parallel turns.

Move Visualization, aerial vectors, emotional state, and physical pain..

Joy

ground & aerial vector

① Puzzlement

② Whump! ..oof!

Pain

③ Thud Pain

Average Wall Ride

9

How to Start Skating...

Rule #1 Don't buy **New Skates!** Yet! Rent and/or buy used 'till you get semi-competant be-cause... Ⓐ You don't know what a "good skate" is... & Ⓑ You don't know what a "bad skate" is. You _will_. If you rent you can try out a bunch of different styles & brands and, coupled with some skating experience you'll begin to get a real feel for what fits your needs.

Rule #2 - Wear a shitload of pads plus a real good helmet!! You _will_ be falling a lot, occasionally on your butt, an area many beginners forget to protect. Used hockey girdles or concealable padded shorts work great!

Hockey Girdle

Rule #3 - Get some basic instruction from an actual human instructor. Books are great but nothing beats hands-on person to person skating experience!

Rule #4 - Find a smooth, relatively clean, relatively traffic & criminal-free parking lot and stay the #!x?; off **Hills**...ramps, slopes, inclines, "itty bitty hills", etc. If you get smushed by a car or shredded on a hill you will then have to unlearn "crash phobia syndrome" **before** you can resume learning non-traumatic skating skills. Some fear (healthy respect) can keep you safe but **excessive fear** can keep you **off** your skates.

Rule #5 - Learn to stop and/or Bail Out FIRST, before you skate one inch! As you learn to move and turn, you'll be **amazed** how quickly you can get into **deep do-do** on inline skates!

Rule #6 - Assume Th' Position! This is definitely the mega rule, the Key to learning and surviving the learning process of inline skating! ① Knees well bent, ② upper torso bent forward, ③ Nose over toes, ④ Eyes ahead, judging terrain, ⑤ hands low in front (see Sight picture), ⑥ Head-knees-toes in line, weight over toes, ⑦ (see diagram) ⑧ (see diagram), ⑨ upper body "quiet" (zero imput). Body coil (knees, back bent) keeps you in position to jump, dyno-lean, tuck, etc. Also a excellent shock-absorber!

hey.. Not Bad!

Aiiieee!

Bong!

Lissen up, maggot!

First Learning Experience

Boosh!

Thock!

④ Eyes ahead.

③ Nose over toes!

② Upper body flexed over toes

① Knees Bent

Correct Sight Picture

Hands Knees Toes

⑤ Hands in front, in view!

⑥ A, B, C - "Head-Knee Toe Line"

⑦ Feet shoulder-wide, slightly scissored

⑧ Toe weighted, wt. distribution 50/50

13

Rule # 7 ("Cool Rule")- Please skate courteously and try to be cool with the po-lice. Whenever you've got skates on you're an ambassador from *Planet Inline!* How you choose to act affects all of us; cool=access, uncool= access *denied!*

Rule #8- Find a group of experienced skaters to recreate with. You'll learn more, **faster** if you're hangin' with other skaters... you'll have more fun too! Books are great but nothing beats skater to skater hands-on interaction.

mornin'

Hey YOU! No Skatin' heah Anytime! Lessee some I.D.!

?!?...

Empty those pockets Right NOW!!

Actual Incident

Rule #9- Subscribe to **Inline** Magazine*! Once I quit falling down a lot and began to learn some actual skills and techniques, Inline's "Demo" section was absolutely invaluable as a source of solid, plain-spoken "skills" information! Plus, there's lots of cultural stuff about all the various tribes of inline skating. Even stuff for pinhead cruisers like me! Excellent!

Rule #10- Have too much **fun**! Break some rules...

* Unsolicited & uncompensated endorsement...

Beginning Skating Made Incredibly Simple...

① Skate in The Position..

② Think in three dimensions* and visualize potential moves as circles and parts thereof.. (Arcs, cuts)

③ SKATE your ASS OFF! The more hours you log on skates, the more your body will automatically learn ("body knowledge"). Instruction, books, etc. are no substitute for actual skating experience! Learning to move on skates over varied terrain is the best teacher of all!

④ Learn to fall well! You're gonna fall, probably a lot, so you may as well get good at it...

grin

Think 3-D, move in Arcs and circles..

Eyes and brain out front!

Vector

feet shoulder wide and scissored

Potential move

Potential move

How To Fall Badly..

Youch!

Ach!

*!@?

oof!

Falls are never a lot of fun but there are lots of ways to reduce pain and injury.

Uncontrolled Fall

*Actually, four dimensions (plus "time")!

pendejo

Here's what really bad body position looks like (just before the buttfall!): (A) Weight heelward, zero control, (B) feet un-staggered, very unstable forward and backward, (C) knees locked; no shock absorption, weight centered on heels, (D) upper torso unflexed, spine straight; less suspension, more weight on heels, (E) Arms flailing wildly, providing no balance and out of position to catch a frontfall, (F) Head literally over heels, eyes on feet... fixing to do a serious buttgrind. Also, since the body is using "skeletal suspension" instead of "muscular suspension", he'll have to reposition and flex before he can initiate movement and/or react to obstacles. Beginners unconciously drift into this stance because: (1) skeletal suspension allows tired muscles to rest, and (2) the brain wants to distance itself from physical threat so the head is pulled back, unfortunately increasing the threat by weighting the heels...

"Anchor Points" * Before "The Position" gets instinctive (body memory) you will have to visually align your various body parts into the correct points in space:
(A)(B)(C) - head-knee-toe alignment, weight toeward, (D) knees well flexed, (which naturally keeps weight off heels!) (E) torso flexed forward, (F) hands/arms quiet, balancing and ready to check a fall. Now, whenever you feel flakey and out of control, slow down and visually check your anchor point configuration and correct as necessary... SOLID!

"The Position" Schematic

"Anchor Points" A-F

Yike!

* physical points of reference

16

gonna die gonna die aiiieee!

Awk!

yeek!

Yo!

Passive Skaters

Head back, weight on heels (fear), **reacting** to conditions, operating **below** skill level, out of "stance" ("The Position") out of control, No grin and very impure thoughts!

Aggressive Skater

Operating at or slightly above skill level, weight on **toes** (in control), using "The Position", slightly tucked, acting with/on the terrain, Not **reacting** to it!! Pure thoughts, big grin...

It can't be over-stressed that "You drive your skates or they drive **you**!"... on skates, at speed, if you're only reacting you're always gonna be a couple steps **behind** the "decision horizon". As a result you begin to lose control, get Nervous and, likely, begin to drift out of "The Position"; pulling your head back, weighting your heels, losing even more control. This is a Negative feedback loop.. a real-time vicious cycle..

Aggressive

Passive

How To Skate Aggressively *

You are here.

Your brain is here.

Decision Horizon

① Skate "Extreme" (for you); always try to work at the edge of your ability - "extreme" is incremental... work "up" slowly! ② Dress for success! Wear enough body armour so you're not anxious about the pain consequences of an attempted move gone wrong. ③ Try to always think at least one move ahead. ④ Remember to have fun! Lots of self-teachers are way too harsh on their students (namely themselves). A certain degree of dedication is required to progress in your skating. However, if you're starting to bash yourself repeatedly (physically & mentally) trying to learn a new move, it might be time to try something new and/or simply take a break. Pain can be a great teacher but it is not required that we become masochists to learn to skate. The main thing is to maintain learning "flow", skate a lot, and enjoy yourself immensley! [see "Learning Curve", pg. 68]

* and "relative" as well...

* Actual "Aggressive" Skating

Note bandages!

18

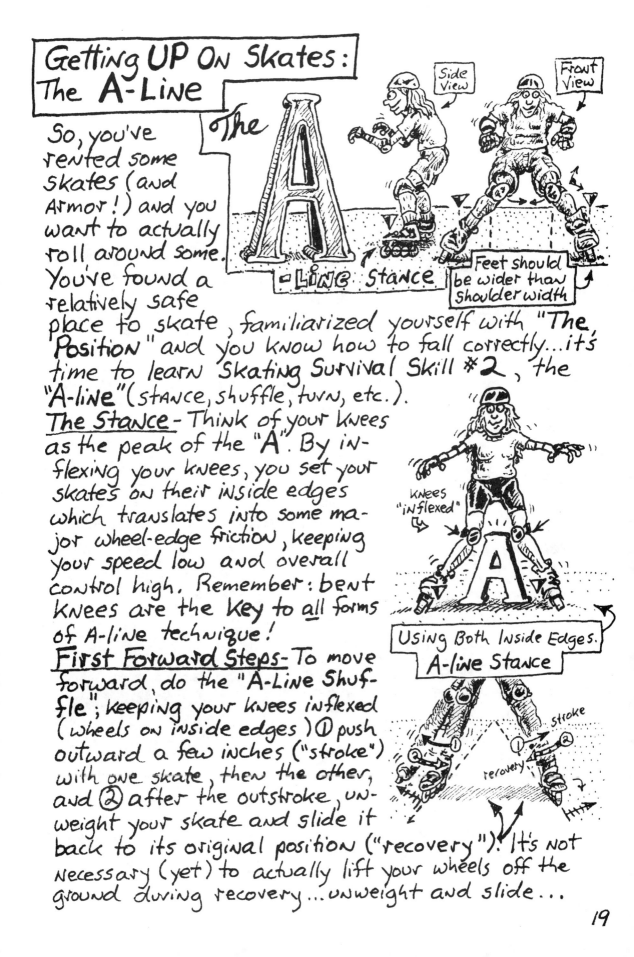

Getting UP On Skates: The A-Line

So, you've rented some skates (and Armor!) and you want to actually roll around some. You've found a relatively safe

The A-Line Stance

Side View   Front View

Feet should be wider than shoulder width

place to skate, familiarized yourself with "**The Position**" and you know how to fall correctly...it's time to learn Skating Survival Skill #2, the "A-line" (stance, shuffle, turn, etc.).

<u>The Stance</u> - Think of your knees as the peak of the "A". By in-flexing your knees, you set your skates on their inside edges which translates into some major wheel-edge friction, keeping your speed low and overall control high. Remember: bent knees are the key to all forms of A-line technique!

knees "inflexed"

Using Both Inside Edges. A-line Stance

<u>First Forward Steps</u> - To move forward, do the "A-Line Shuffle"; keeping your knees inflexed (wheels on inside edges) ① push outward a few inches ("stroke") with one skate, then the other, and ② after the outstroke, un-weight your skate and slide it

stroke
recovery

back to its original position ("recovery"). It's not necessary (yet) to actually lift your wheels off the ground during recovery...unweight and slide...

19

...your skate back to its original position. Repeat on the other side.

Oh yeah!

Forward Stroke

"recovery"

Note the weighting indicators (▽) & weight shift pattern.. it will make sense SOON!

This looks extremely complicated but so would a description of walking. It is just like walking except you're wearing a funny costume, balanced on wobbly skates, & trying to figure out what an "inside edge" IS!? To add to your growing bafflement, your skate wheels may be rounded but they have "edges"!* Anyhow, you're in the "A-line position", on your (trust me) inside edges, doing alternating "outstrokes" to kind of push yourself along without falling on your ass... your toes should be angled out a little which is why this is sometimes called the "duck walk". As your ability to propel yourself forward improves, your stance will narrow and evolve into the "forward shuffle" then, eventually, the "forward stroke".

oh my gawd...

I'm doin' it!!

A-line Shuffle

* See pg. 40

20

Staying UP On Skates...

Stability On Skates; Where It Comes From, How To Get Some...

It's time to get a little mechanistic *: there are two types of Inline Skate Stability — "long axis" (front to back) and "short axis" (side to side)...

whaa!

Unstable

Very Stable

2 mph   15 mph

Velocity Increases Stability!

Short Axis Stability and Width Of Stance

very stable at med. to high speeds!

Wide Stance - "A-Line" very stable side to side, maximum edge friction; relatively slow...

Normal Stance Feet shoulder-wide fairly stable side/side, minor edge friction relatively fast...

In Line Stance Skates virtually in line - stance width 1" to 4"! minimum edge friction, very fast...

At slow speeds you need a relatively wide stance to keep your balance. As speed increases, kinetic energy increases, which gives you "inertial stability" along your vector. In other words,

Yike!

FOOM!

wide stance

narrow stance

The Faster You Go, The More Stable You Become!

Newton's First Law: An object in motion <u>tends</u> to move in a straight line (inertia). [Apologies to Sir Isaac Newton]

As velocity increases, energy increases, ∴ inertia increases...

* And "scientistic" as well!

21

As well as "inertial stability", your **angular momentum** increases as speed increases. This is meaningful in that if you're going real fast and lose control, you'll (hopefully) tend to fall and slide with the **curve of the earth** and dissipate the fall energy gradually in the form of friction (heat) instead of breaking bones!

High Speed Butt Slide — Same fall distance (36"), but fall forces get spread over a longer distance...less pain!

— — — — 36" — — —

damn!

YOW!

ouch! ouch! ouch!

CRUNCH!

Angular momentum

Low Speed Buttfall — Short distance, big fall force...Big Pain!!

zero Angular momentum

Along with inertial stability at high speeds, your eight spinning wheels give you, in effect, **eight tiny gyroscopes,** the torque of which also work against a sideways fall. The gyroscopic effect is small but highly meaningful in that,

if you <u>want</u> lots of speed you'll have to reduce rolling friction by narrowing your stance as well as staggering your skates longways to increase your front-to-back stability.

Yaaa-hooo!

Inertial Stability

WOOOSH!

Angular momentum

gyroscopic stability

Long Stance

See next page →

"Length" of Stance

At **low speeds** and when you're just messin' around on skates a "short" wide stance is OK — it gives you high maneuverability and lots of side to side stability... [①, below]

As your speed increases (like when you're **cruising** around) you'll want to get in the **habit** of **staggering** your skates for maximum front-to-back stability in case you hit a rock, catch an edge or otherwise get unexpectedly **destabilized**. [②,③ below]

Long Axis Stability

check it out!   whoa!

Unstable   Short Stance

yow!

Force

Very Stable   Long Narrow Stance

① **Short & wide stance** — low to med. speeds, highly maneuverable

② **Longer Stance** — skates staggered but still about a shoulderwidth apart. Stable at any speed and fairly maneuverable

③ **Long Narrow Stance** — skates literally in line! minimal edge friction, very long stability footprint. Medium to very high speeds. Low maneuverability! A.k.a. "long stance"

To Summerize: Your stability on skates comes from your width of stance, **length** of stance and how you "fit" your stance to your velocity!

23

☆Caution — the Forward Shuffle and Stroke descriptions below are for definition ONLY...don't try ☆ either yet...

Forward Shuffle

Forward Stroke

Like the A-line Shuffle, the Forward Shuffle is also a minimal, short push-out stroke done by shifting weight from skate to skate, toes out slightly. Known also as the "Frankenstein Walk", this "stroke" uses your center edges initially...

This advanced stroke is done by alternating "pushing out" strokes as well. It is different in that ① your stance is narrow, ② your skates are mainly parallel (not toes-out), and ③ the "outstroke" involves much greater power and extension than the A-line or Forward Shuffle.

Now, back to the "A-line Shuffle"; assuming that you're able to propel yourself forward, eventually you will need to change directions or "Turn"...

A-line Turns Done by simply shifting your weight from skate to skate, turning opposite the shift... weight to right foot, turn left...weight to left, go right.*

*Important Terminology/Concept- "Opposite Direction Foot" or "O.D.F." To simplify descriptions of complex moves coming up, the "foot-you-weight-to-turn-the-other-way" will heretofore be referred to as the "O.D.F." ➤

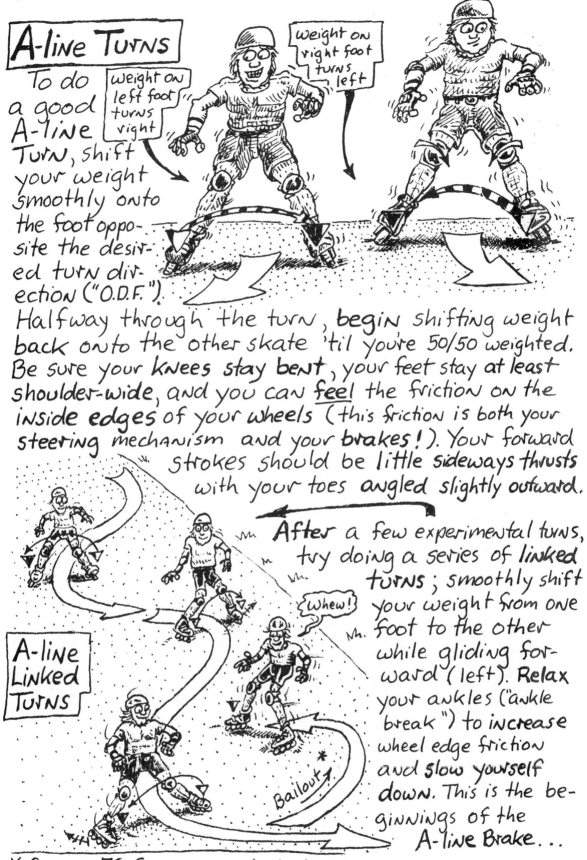

A-line Turns

To do a good A-line Turn, shift your weight smoothly onto the foot opposite the desired turn direction ("O.D.F.").

weight on left foot turns right

weight on right foot turns left

Halfway through the turn, begin shifting weight back onto the other skate 'til you're 50/50 weighted. Be sure your **knees stay bent**, your feet stay at least shoulder-wide, and you can <u>feel</u> the friction on the **inside edges** of your wheels (this friction is both your steering mechanism and your **brakes!**). Your forward strokes should be little sideways thrusts with your toes angled slightly outward.

After a few experimental turns, try doing a series of **linked turns**; smoothly shift your weight from one foot to the other while gliding forward (left). **Relax your ankles** ("ankle break") to increase wheel edge friction and **slow yourself down**. This is the beginnings of the A-line Brake...

A-line Linked Turns

Whew!

Bailout

*See pg. 76 for more on bailouts...

25

A-line Brake To slow and stop in the A-line position, you've got to; ① widen your stance to maximize wheel edge friction, ② relax and lower your body and angle your toes out slightly. These actions alone **should** slow you significantly! ③ As your stance widens, "break" your ankles to let your skates tilt further onto the inside edges (see "Broken Ankle Brake", page 38). If this major friction doesn't stop you, angle your toes out a little more and/or try squeezing your legs back together with your ankles remaining "broken". If this doesn't stop you, see below! Caution: when you're learning this and other braking methods, always work at slow speeds, relax your body and avoid inclines.

Lower your body

Angle of Ankle "break"

Widen Stance

"break"

Ankle Straight   Ankle "Broken"

Basic A-line Bailout IF the regular stopping protocol (above) fails to stop you in time, shift weight to one foot ("O.D.F.") and initiate a turn. Use your edges (now angling against your vector, white arrow) to push outside the turn while continuing to relax your ankles and knees (and lowering your body). If you don't stop NOW, relax even more and **crumple to the ground.**

(damn!)

26

Basic Forward Stroke

Once you've mastered the A-line Shuffle, bring your legs in until your wheels are perpendicular to the pavement, onto your "center" edges. To start your feet should be slightly toes-out & just over shoulder-width apart (✪, below). Keep your knees bent and your weight forward in the boot ("toe weighted").

A-Line Shuffle

Basic Forward Shuffle

Stance Width and Skill Level...

A-Line

"parallel"

Key- ⫶⫶⫶ - Beginner
⫶∴ - Novice *
≡ - Intermediate
⫽⫽ - Advanced To Expert

→ ← ↓ Stance Narrowing

← As your forward stroke improves you'll notice that your feet naturally get closer & closer together; your stance "narrows". A narrower stance creates the least stroke friction and improves muscle efficiency. Experts zoom along on a 4" wide ribbon of pavement!

* Novice - A beginner with a little experience...

↰ Use alternating short outstrokes to slowly propel yourself forward. Try to add in a little "glide" between the outstrokes. As your "shuffle" improves to "stroking", your strokes get longer, stronger, and the glide interval increases. The most important thing is to keep your knees bent (!) and go only as fast as your primitive stopping ability can handle (!!). Frequently scan for your "anchor points" to be certain you're in the proper body/limb configuration ("Sight Picture", next pg.). Concentrate on smooth movement, keeping a quiet upper body, and...

.. and good form. **Never** skate with your eyes locked on your feet(!). **Do** scan your toe-knee-head alignment frequently to maintain optimal body configuration (left).

"Sight Picture" and "Scan"...

① **Body Position:** Ⓐ hands in sight so your upper body is fairly quiet (not flailing) & you're prepared to fall, Ⓑ & Ⓒ your knees are over your toes which indicates that your knees are actually <u>bent</u> and your weight is, ipso facto, toeward, ② **Decision Horizon** * your mini<u>mum</u> braking/evasion distance .. the imaginary line where potentiality becomes actuality according to velocity ("middle distance"). Your Decision Horizon gets closer as your skills impro<u>ve</u>!

③ **Actual Horizon** - Obviously you want to know what's going on ahead of you so you can plan your future moves, route changes, etc. Once good technique gets hard-wired in the body knowledge circuits (instinctualized), you'll check your anchor points (①) only when you start feeling out of control. The main thing is to always be aware of your surroundings; near, far, front, sides, back, etc.

Hey! I got my hand right!

click!

Learning Tip #27 Whenever you're practicing a new skill or polishing up an old skill, keep a strong **mental image** of the ideal form you're working toward. You'll experience a mental "**click**" whenever your flailing body corresponds with parts of the ideal form. When you're clickin' <u>on all the ideal points</u>, you're an ideal skatin' dude!

Move Visualization

*A.k.a. "Event Horizon"

Doin' th' "Linda Blair"

In order to be aware of your **total environment**, it's necessary to constantly look behind you when skating on the street in traffic. Unless done correctly, looking backwards can literally torque you off your feet and/or create major instability at a very bad time ... thus, the "Linda Blair:" the ability to glance backward without losing control by torso-torquing your skates...

"Combat Aircraft Pilot Terminology

eech!

huh?

Bluehair*! skate for your life!

Good Form: ① upper body preturned so skater glances back without twisting body ② Eye rotation minimizes head rotation, ③ skates scissored!

Good Evasive Tactics help too!

Bad Form - twisting upper torso abruptly to look back..

Awk!

Ask me about my Grandchildren

① Turn head 90°, eyes rotate back...
② Eyes forward quickly, slowly rotate head to front!

The "Linda Blair," Back view

*"bluehair-" little old lady steering a great big car...

29

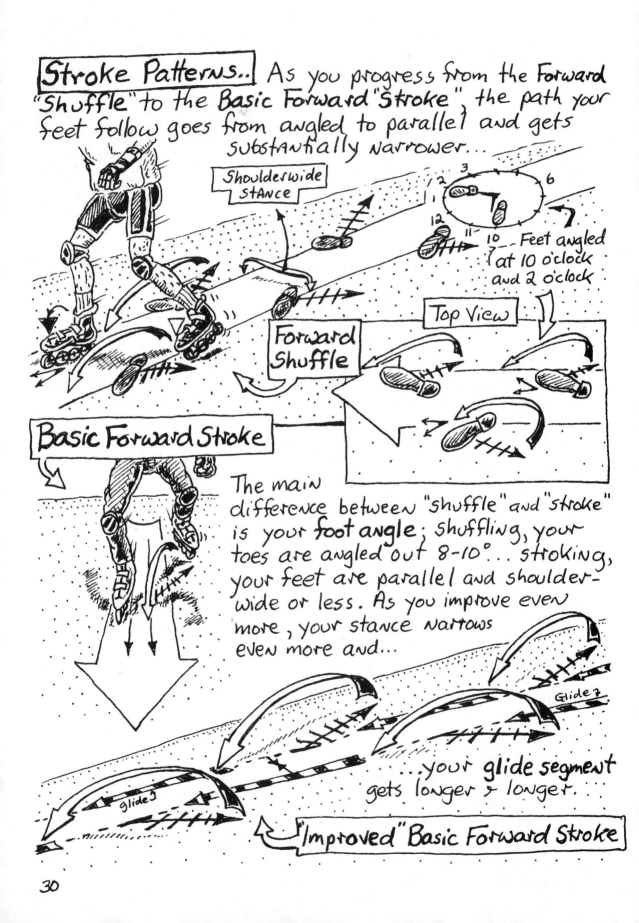

Stroke Patterns.. As you progress from the Forward "Shuffle" to the Basic Forward "Stroke" the path your feet follow goes from angled to parallel and gets substantially narrower...

Shoulderwide stance

Feet angled at 10 o'clock and 2 o'clock

Top View

Forward Shuffle

Basic Forward Stroke

The main difference between "shuffle" and "stroke" is your **foot angle**; shuffling, your toes are angled out 8-10°... stroking, your feet are parallel and shoulderwide or less. As you improve even more, your stance narrows even more and...

Glide

glide

...your **glide segment** gets longer & longer.

"Improved" Basic Forward Stroke

Glide* As you get better at forward stroking, begin adding short "glide segments" between strokes. Gliding feels good, gives your legs a micro-rest and makes a choppy, effortful move sequence smooth and _graceful_! In short, gliding teaches **timing** and timing perfects your stroke! For every 20 strokes a beginner takes, an expert skater will take 4 or 5 evenly spaced, smooth and powerful strokes!

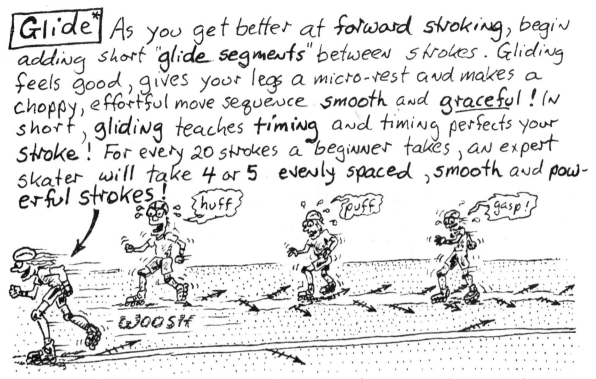

The "trick" here is **economy of movement**. As your balance, timing, and general coordination on skates improves (mainly a function of net time-on-skates) you'll be thrashing around less, moving your body for power (not for balance), and doing a lot less work! Once you've learned the two-legged glide interval between strokes, try gliding short distances on one foot, the other after the next stroke. [hint- you only have to lift your off skate an inch or so off the ground].

Once you learn to glide on one foot while stroking, **congratulations!** You're now on the lifelong path to **Inline Nirvana**, the eternal quest to achieve the **perfect forward stroke!**

* "Riding the Roll"

Swizzle

The Swizzle is arguably the most important of the learning "strokes"; you learn about wheel "edges", friction "speed bleeds", as well as knee swing / skate tilt interaction. You also learn the rudiments of "smearing," the art of making inline wheels do arcs & turns while staying in contact with the ground! For example (below); when you begin the outstroke you "swing" your knees apart which rotates your toes out and rolls your wheels from inside edges to their outside edges. This toe-in / toe-out rotation on the pavement is a minor "smear" which creates additional wheel edge friction. Just like the A-line swizzle, the regular swizzle can be used to regulate your overall speed (friction "governor") as well as to come to a complete stop. [See "Swizzle Stops", see pg. 37]. This is a good way to stop* because you are using big leg muscles to "absorb" speed!

Out-stroke

OUTSIDE EDGES

Instroke

INSIDE EDGES

OUTSIDE EDGES

Out-stroke

Instroke

OUTSIDE EDGES

INSIDE EDGES

Yippie ti Yo!

ED

Using Outside Edges on the Instroke, Then Using Knee Rotation ("Swing") to Begin the Outstroke

*At slower speeds ONLY!

Elementary A-line Swizzle

To "A-line Swizzle", keep your skates tilted on their **inside edges** and alternately **squeeze in** and **shove out** to create a wide, continuous hourglass skate path. Unlike regular swizzling (shown below) wherein you're using alternating <u>inside</u> and outside edges, here you stay on inside edges throughout to maximize **wheel edge friction**. The A-line Swizzle is probably better as a speed-control/braking method than as a means of forward propulsion due to the friction it creates.

Squeeze

Out

IN

Out

IN

"shove"

quack quack!

"Normal" Swizzle

OUT

IN

OUT

IN

Swizzle "Stroke" schematic ↑

Duck Walk

The regular swizzle, like the "duckwalk," is a great way to propel yourself forward & backward. The main difference from the A-line version is that you're using both inside <u>and</u> outside edges!

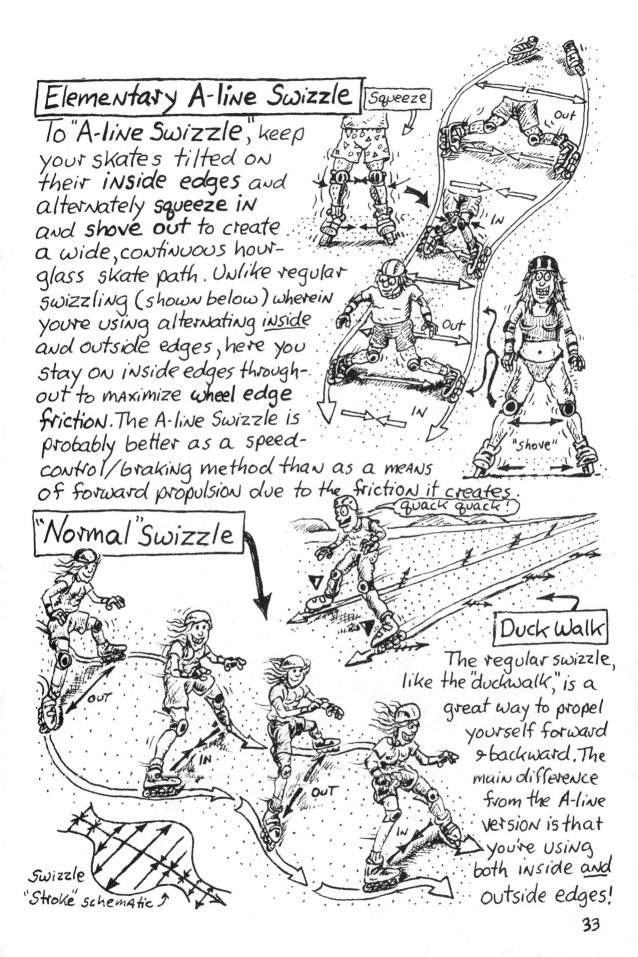

33

Swizziology 101:
Knee Swing / Skate
Tilt Steering & Some
Stuff About Relevant
Muscle
Groups

Standing stationary, rotate your knees out. Notice your feet rotate out "following" the knee rotation out (abductor muscle group).

Rotate your knees in... this also rotates your toes in (adductor muscle group).

muscle group location

Abductor Rotation (knees out) | Adductor Rotation (knees in)

Rolling on skates and rotating your knees in and out will result in a **Swizzle***! When swizzling you're using your knees in "opposition" (in/in, out/out, in/in, etc.) using inside edges going inward and outside edges going outward...

...to gain momentum or to lose speed by "smearing" your wheels to create friction.

"outside"   "inside"

right foot

Knee rotations ("swings") are the foundation of inline skate control & steering!

* width of swizzle exaggerated for illustrative purposes!

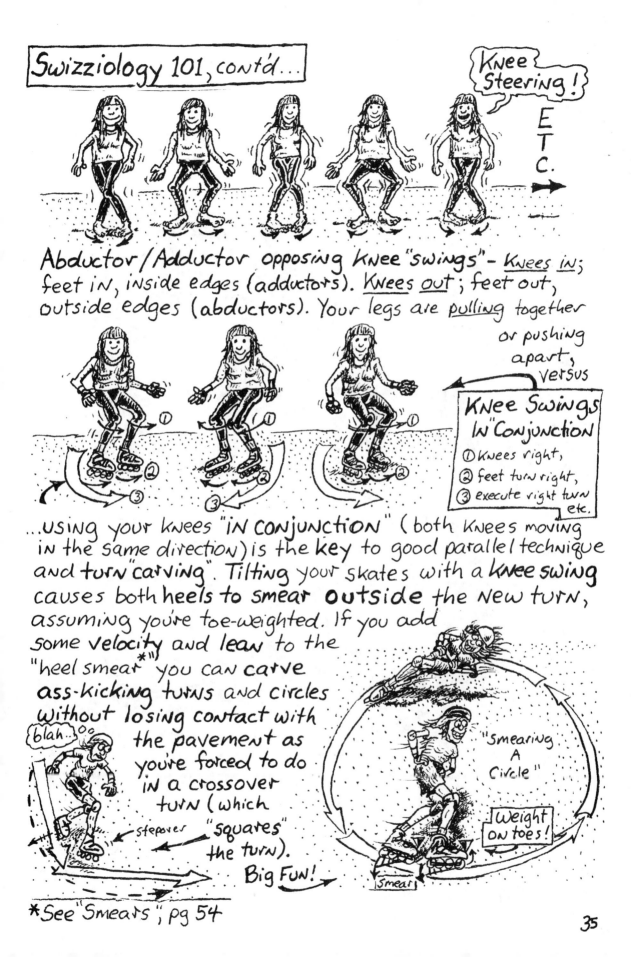

Swizziology 101, cont'd...

Knee Steering!

E T C.

Abductor/Adductor opposing knee "swings" - knees in; feet in, inside edges (adductors). Knees out; feet out, outside edges (abductors). Your legs are pulling together or pushing apart, versus

Knee Swings In "Conjunction"
① knees right,
② feet turn right,
③ execute right turn etc.

...using your knees "in conjunction" (both knees moving in the same direction) is the key to good parallel technique and turn "carving". Tilting your skates with a knee swing causes both heels to smear outside the new turn, assuming you're toe-weighted. If you add some velocity and lean to the "heel smear*" you can carve ass-kicking turns and circles without losing contact with the pavement as you're forced to do in a crossover turn (which "squares" the turn).

blah...

stepover

"Big Fun!"

"smearing A circle"

Weight on toes!

smear

*See "Smears", pg 54

35

Swizzle → Sculling

While "swizzling" is defined here as symmetrical **grounded** "push-strokes" in an hourglass pattern, swizzle techniques can be used to "scull"; grounded asymmetrical IN-outstrokes using inside-outside edges for propulsion...

One Foot Sculling ("Fishtail")

Crossunder Sculling (see "Crossunder/Crossover")

Grounded Forward Strokes

Narrow Stance

"Scull" Stroking

Offset Swizzle Sculling

"Recovery"

Wide Stance

The most difficult & complex sculling technique is the "Backwards Crossunder Turn" [see pg. 145]

Sculling is a great technique for skating narrow paths and tweezing through pedestrian hazards in constricted areas. Good speed control too!

Swizzle Stops You've got two static-stop options: the "Toes Out" Stop or the "Toes In" Stop ("snowplow stop"). You can also bleed off speed with a "bailout spin" (bottom center) prior to the actual stop.

whew!

Toes Out - Very slow speeds only!!! On the out-stroke, simply freeze your leg muscles to counteract the outward motion of your skates. If you fail to counteract the outward skate motion you'll execute one of the most dreaded "falls" imaginable*... Swizzle Splits!

! ! ! !
o ! !oof! !
o ! ! ! !

Toes Out Stop

Swizzle Splits ⟩ Yow!

Toes In Stop Similar to a Toes Out Stop without the conse-quences... you're doing a muscle freeze against angled-in skates to come to a quick stop. Slow Speeds Only!! You can do a toe-toe T-stop* but it's not necessary to bring your feet together

Scheit!?

Also known as the "snowplow stop"

.1 mph

Click!

Speed Bleed

2 mph

Toes In Stop

T-Stop on a Bailout Spin (optional)

Face Plant Result of a T-stop before you've slowed to a near stop..

*It's a guy thing...

★For more on T-stops see pg. 61

37

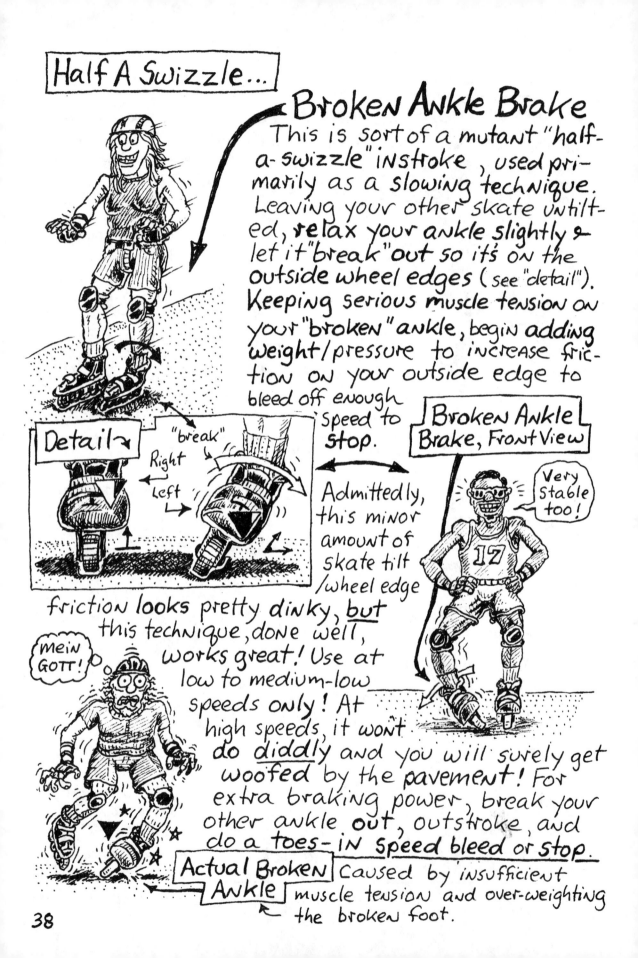

Half A Swizzle...

Broken Ankle Brake

This is sort of a mutant "half-a-swizzle" instroke, used primarily as a slowing technique. Leaving your other skate untilted, **relax** your ankle slightly & let it "break" **out** so it's on the outside wheel edges (see "detail"). Keeping serious muscle tension on your "broken" ankle, begin **adding weight/pressure** to increase friction on your outside edge to bleed off enough speed to **stop.**

Detail "break"
Right
Left

Broken Ankle Brake, Front View

Very stable too!

17

Admittedly, this minor amount of skate tilt /wheel edge friction looks pretty dinky, **but** this technique, done well, works great! Use at low to medium-low speeds only! At high speeds, it won't **do diddly** and you will surely get **woofed** by the pavement! For extra braking power, break your other ankle **out**, outstroke, and do a **toes-in** speed bleed or **stop.**

mein GOTT!

Actual Broken Ankle Caused by insufficient muscle tension and over-weighting the broken foot.

38

Introduction To Edges, Boot Weighting, and Dr. Spasm...

Inline Skates, technically speaking, vant to move in a **straight line.** Der "rolling resistance" of ze tiny vehicle is **least** on ze long axis; thus, it vill travel in a straight line indefinitely, until acted upon to **force** it from a straight path...

long → axis

short axis

Dr. Spasm, PhD

...but, our skating universe is **curvilinear!** Zo, how de heck do ve go about making der **gottdam** things _not_ **go straight?!** Ze long answer involves a complex interwoven system of musculo-skeletal input, surface cohesion, velocity, centrifugal force, weight shifts, and skate wheel characteristics. **Ach!** Ze short answer iss _edges_!

Like snow skis, your **rounded** skate wheels have **edges.** Tilting the wheels on edge _makes_ the skate **turn**...

Edges

Snow Ski

Skate wheel

Right Edge

Left Edge

Lean the right ski onto its left edge and it **tracks** left. Tilt onto its right edge, turn right. Leave it flat ("center edge") and it **tracks** straight. **Visualize edges** on your **skate wheels**... right edge goes **right,** left edge **left,** and **straight** on the **center edge.**

Rt

L

40

...So, just like a ski, leaning your skate onto its edge causes it to turn. Henceforth, leaning onto edges will be referred to as "tilt". Tilt is created by applying pressure to a specific zone on the sole of the boot (next page). Applying pressure (or weight) on the skate's toe or heel affects the skate's up/down "attitude". Pressure on the toes raises (or "un-weights" the heel, pressure back towards the heel raises the toe wheel. A skate on one wheel turns very easily. This is a pivot turn* There are lots of ways to affect skate tilt and attitude. Knee swings, upper body torque (below) and by applying spot pressure on the sole of the boot ("weighting the boot"). Upper body torque can be applied to force your skates into a turn but it's kinda like using dynamite to fish...a waste of energy and a bit risky. As a beginner, you want to keep your upper body quiet so you don't torque yourself off balance! Finesse beats force in skating so you might want to learn boot weighting initially & body torque later.

right edge, right turn

center edge, straight

left edge, left turn

Foot Flexion & Toe weighting to turn right

① Upper body torques to the right...

② which rotates the hips to the right...

③ ..which twists the legs clockwise...

④ ..which forces toes around to the right.

* More on the pivot turn, pg. 53

41

"Foot Finesse"... various forms

up ↑   ↓ down

Foot Flexion

Outside   Inside   ## Ankle Twisting

Leg and upper body FORCE

⇓ inside edge

↓↓↓ toes

▨ ball of foot

⇓⇓ outside edge

Accupressure Points of the Sole!

"Weighting the boot" means basically applying **spot pressure** (and/or body weight) on points and zones on the sole of the boot using **toe pressure, foot flexion** and/or **ankle twists**. Gaining good boot weighting abilities requires experience, experiment, and patience. Practice your **in-boot** accupressure technique at very slow speeds on a very **smooth** surface so that you can feel the nuances of **subtle** weight shifts. It's kinda like balancing on a cone on one foot; → you want to keep your body as **still** as possible and do the balancing with **your foot alone**...the less upper body imput the better!

＊ Shaded arrows correspond to "Accupressure" diagram...

42

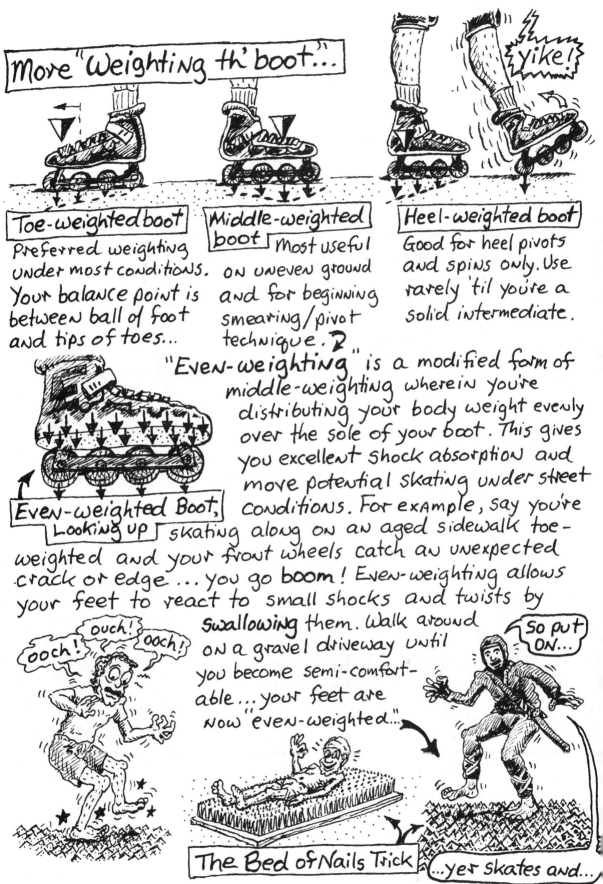

More "Weighting th' boot..."

yike!

Toe-weighted boot
Preferred weighting under most conditions. Your balance point is between ball of foot and tips of toes...

Middle-weighted boot Most useful on uneven ground and for beginning smearing/pivot technique.

Heel-weighted boot
Good for heel pivots and spins only. Use rarely 'til you're a solid intermediate.

Even-weighted Boot, Looking up

"Even-weighting" is a modified form of middle-weighting wherein you're distributing your body weight evenly over the sole of your boot. This gives you excellent shock absorption and more potential skating under street conditions. For example, say you're skating along on an aged sidewalk toe-weighted and your front wheels catch an unexpected crack or edge... you go **boom!** Even-weighting allows your feet to react to small shocks and twists by **swallowing** them. Walk around on a gravel driveway until you become semi-comfortable... your feet are now "even-weighted..."

ooch! ouch! ooch!

So put ON...

The Bed of Nails Trick

...yer skates and...

43

Simple Parallel Turns →

...Try this: get going straight at medium slow speed, skates parallel. Now just think "right turn"...most people will make a gentle turn to the right. The point here being that your body instinctively knows what to do. Now get going straight, med. speed, skates parallel...make sure your knees are well bent throughout. Leading with your knees, "knee swing" and put your wheels on edge: Right Turn [rt. foot-outside edge, left foot-inside edge]. The more you angle your edges, the tighter the turn. Now try a "weight shift parallel turn..." moving med. slow, skates parallel & shoulder-wide...smoothly shift your weight onto the O.D.F. * and look into the turn.

"Edge" Turn

Note: scissor your outside skate forward on turns!

You will make a nice gentle turn (hopefully). Try several turns with different weight shift combinations: 60%-40%, 80%-20%, etc. The more weight on the O.D.F., the tighter the turn. Now combine hard edge and weight shift; this is the intermediate level parallel turn!

eyes "leading"

outside
inside

Weight Shift [70-30%]

Hard Edge + Wt. shift ↗

yeee-ha!

Weight Shift Turn

inside ↑
↓ outside

⌷⌷⌷⌷⌷ → = scissor

* "Opposite Direction Foot"

44

Leans, Edges & Centrifugal Force...

Skating anything but a straight line requires the skater to balance **edge** use & **body** movement with **velocity**, **gravity** and **centrifugal force** ("C-force").

The greater the speed the harder the lean and edge pressure to execute the same turn radius as a low speed turn.

outside edge

inside edge

Low speed **parallel** turn to the left

gravity

centrifugal force

gravity

Edge Pushing

High speed **parallel** turn to the left using "hard edges" and a big lean

At higher speeds on a turn you're pushing hard outside on your edges for maximum friction & power to counteract forces pulling you outside the turn (C-force) and down (gravity).

① Soft Edge, Slight Turn

Lean angle

② Hard Edge, Tight Turn

③ stroke & weight

Very Hard Edge, Tighter Turn

The steeper the lean, the harder the edge, the tighter the turn!

45

Centrifugal Forces...

Anybody who has **failed** to execute a speed-appropriate **lean** in a high speed turn has experienced being **flung** out of the "centrifugal bowl"... ouch!

yaaaiiiieee...

wide lip

Width of lip equals margin of error

Short Falling Distance

Velocity

Velocity

Gravity

Centrifugal Bowl (cross section) -medium speed profile-

The **faster** you go, the **greater** the lean required to stay **inside**. Plus, the faster you go, the wider and **taller** the bowl becomes [as well as losing the lip (margin of error)].

yiiiiiiieeee!

oof!

The Wok of Death (high speed)

The faster you go, the higher the lip of the bowl...the **harder** you **fall!**

Over The Lip (of the "Centrifugal Bowl"

At low speeds it's hard to get up to the **rim** (lip), much less to get tossed out. Obviously, the faster you go, the steeper your lean needs to be to stay **inside** the bowl...

yiii!

"Poor dude..."

Although the "bowl" is **imaginary**, it's a way of **seeing** terrain potential when you add speed and **style**. When you see the "**waves**" you can start surfin'! (see **next** page *→)

- mph +

✳ See pg. 150 also...

46

Centrifugal Shape...

If you're only going from point A to point B **fast**, you can afford to see in two dimensions (like the, uh... racerheads.).

Point A

Start

Finish

"INNER SKATING"

Point B

Racerhead "Thought"

However, once you start adding **three dimensionality** to the skating **equation** (ie: get off the straight line with jumps, spins, upper body torque, etc.) the "flat" skating plane starts getting **wavy** and begins to take on **shape**! Then you add **style**...

o O O O

Funhog Skater "Thought"

Stylin'

Vunce ve haf **shape**, ve can haf some real **FUN**!

47

Scissoring This is going from skates side by side & parallel to a longer stance by moving a skate forward. You gain front-to back stability and optimum position for an upcoming turn, spin, or "cross" move.*

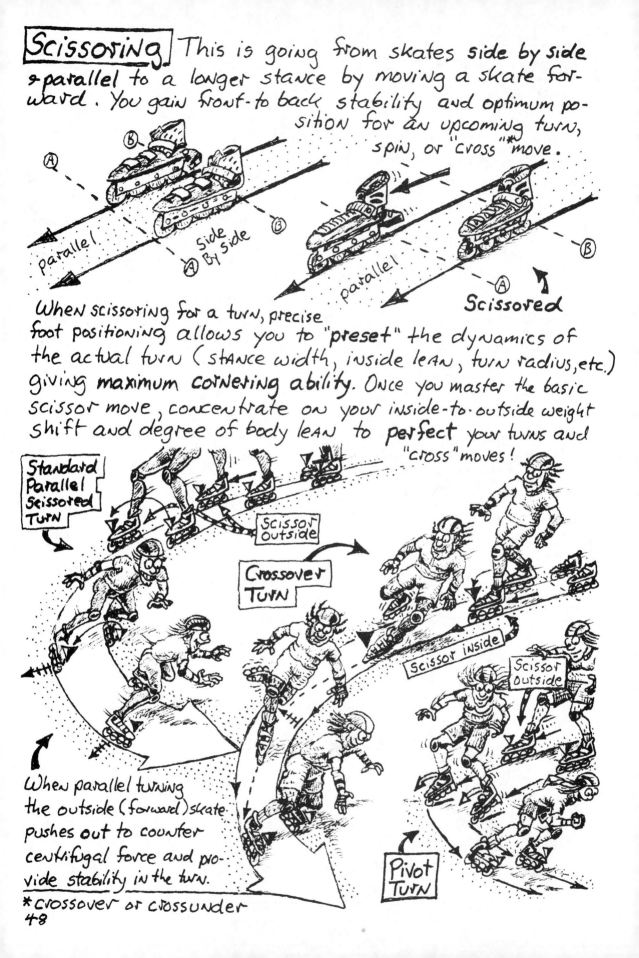

parallel

side by side

parallel

Scissored

When scissoring for a turn, precise foot positioning allows you to "preset" the dynamics of the actual turn (stance width, inside lean, turn radius, etc.) giving maximum cornering ability. Once you master the basic scissor move, concentrate on your inside-to-outside weight shift and degree of body lean to perfect your turns and "cross" moves!

Standard Parallel Scissored Turn

Scissor Outside

Crossover Turn

Scissor Inside

Scissor Outside

When parallel turning the outside (forward) skate pushes out to counter centrifugal force and provide stability in the turn.

Pivot Turn

* crossover or crossunder

48

If you attempt a **sharp turn or spin** with your skates side-by-side or reverse scissored (outside skate back) you will **pretzel*** your legs and **fall big time!**

Skates side-by-side

Awk

Tangleation Detail

Rt

Rt

L

L

meíde!

reversed scissored¹

Oof!

¹ Perfect position for a crossover turn.

Initially beginners should strive to keep the **upper body quiet** and let a slight lean carry them through the arc of the turn. With more experience, add the "preturn" as you scissor and **increase your lean** into the turn: ① scissor; ② preturn, & ③ lean & turn

slight lean

Beginner Turn: ① scissor (no preturn), ③ lean slightly & turn [very "passive" turn]

Advanced Turn: ① scissor, ② preturn, ③ lean & turn ["active" turn]

Dynamic Turn: shift weight to the outside skate as you scissor and use preturn torque to Amp the turn. A hard lean inside gives dramatic performance here!

③ Increase your lean angle and shift more & more weight to outside

* "Tangleation" - pretzeled legs condition

49

Turns and Edges

The more you work your edges by combining leans, power strokes and weight shifts amplified by centrifugal force, the more dynamic and committed your "turn style" becomes. A good place to be dynamic & committed is on **Hills** →

Aiiieee!

Wahoo!

Fall line

Transition - Skates Unweighted

On very steep hills* you can use hard edges and leans to create wheel friction to bleed off speed, taking a zigzag descent line at angles to the fall line (crisp turns, below). The skater going down the fall line and minimizing edge friction will go **much faster** than the hard edge skater (and risks a runaway as well). The slaloming skater moves at a fairly constant speed under control and doesn't risk a runaway from too much acceleration too fast!

Hard edges, hard leans

Gentle Turns

Crisp Turns

"Slalom"

*For more on hills see pg. 101

Turns and Edges...

If you want to do a "hard-edge" turn or maneuver without losing speed from excessive wheel edge friction, do it on ONE FOOT! You keep the high control of the "hard edge" but incur only 50% of the speed bleed debt!

It's a dyno-bargain!

| 100% friction | 50% friction |

Turning on one foot requires some upper leg & torso movement to set the skate on the desired edge

Weight shift to outside edge

Summary

Since we all crave SPEED, it would seem logical to minimize all wheel edge friction at all times & run fast and straight exclusively *. However, this same friction can be put to good use in creating the dynamic arcs and loops of pavement surfing, as well as governing your speed on major downhills to avoid runaways!

Also, when you get into big leans while doing high speed arcs and turns, wheel edge friction is what keeps you securely fastened to the planet!! Some other easy ways to turn are...

Hot damn!

"Bombing"

Surfin'

Foom

| fastest | slowest |

* "Bombing" (downhill)

51

Toe-drag Turn/Spin

You can drag a toe wheel to create drag/friction to turn in the drag direction (example - drag right toe wheel, turn to the right). Make the turn a spin by holding the toe-drag 'til you come around a full 180°. Begin at slow speeds only & practice until you can do a full 360° (below).

① Pre-turn your upper body and drag the toe wheel

② Shift additional weight onto the toe wheel and use it for stability as you come around.

③ If you want to spin past 180°, weight the heel of the other skate...

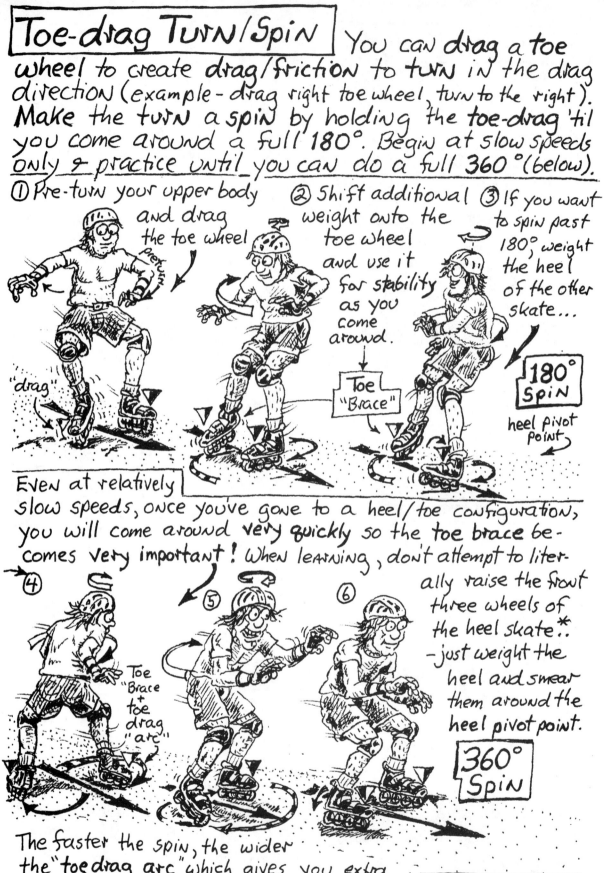

"preturn"

"drag"

Toe "Brace"

180° Spin

heel pivot point

Even at relatively slow speeds, once you've gone to a heel/toe configuration, you will come around very quickly so the toe brace becomes very important! When learning, don't attempt to literally raise the front three wheels of the heel skate.* - just weight the heel and smear them around the heel pivot point.

④ Toe "Brace" + toe drag "arc"

⑤

⑥

360° Spin

The faster the spin, the wider the "toe drag arc" which gives you extra stability on the outside of the spin...

* See ③, above

52

Basic Pivot Turn-

This is the method used to make an **angular turn** instead of a curvey one... it's also the **gateway** skill for a lot of advanced moves!

Scissor: ↦↦↦↦↦

① Preturn
②} Rotate knees
③} and pivot on toes

Beginning Form-

Ⓐ- Going slow & parallel, scissor forward the skate opposite the direction of the turn-to-be. Ⓑ- Pivot toe-weighted* 45-90° and make a "square" turn. Ⓒ- Scissor the other skate forward** and turn right (diagram). Note that the scissor keeps your legs untangled on the turn...unless you did it backwards!

yeek!

Advanced Form

Here you begin to use some upper body movement (not torque, yet!) in the "preturn."

First, scissor as usual and Ⓓ- turn your upper body so you're facing the turn direction(①), pivot up on your toes 45°- 90° and swing your knees around(②&③) to follow your upper body around the corner. Add a little upper-body torque as you become better at doing the move.

reverse scissor

* When learning, **smear**! keep your wheels grounded.
** Always train new moves bilaterally

Pivot & Smeared Turns

There are two ways to cause an inline skate to make a **curve**: the **Pivot** (below, left) - putting a skate (or skates) up on **toe** or **heel** wheels and turning the skate in the air, or the **Smear** (below, rt.) - pivoting your skates with all 8 wheels on the ground. **Smearing** is a great *speed-bleed technique!*

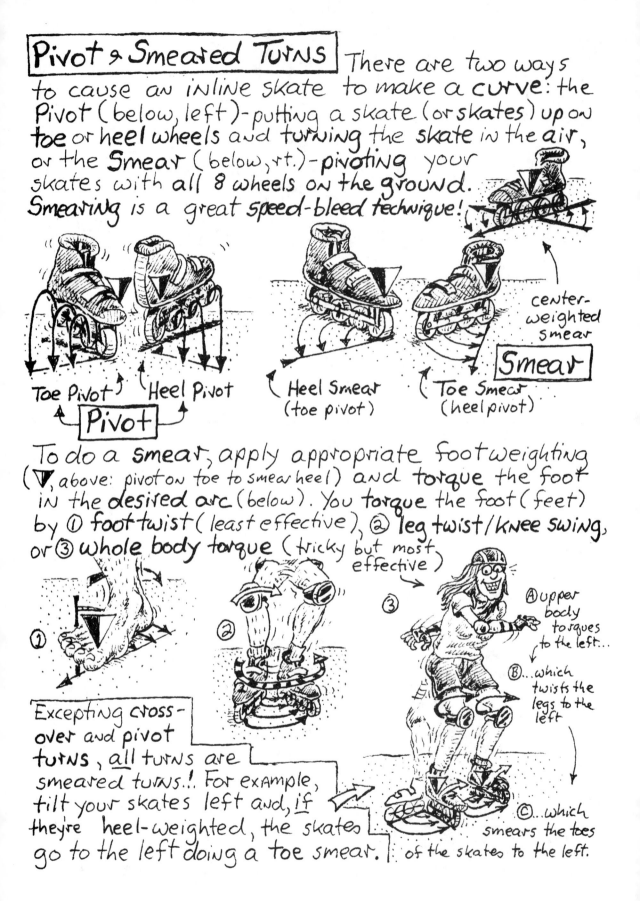

center-weighted smear

Toe Pivot → ← Heel Pivot

Pivot

Heel Smear (toe pivot)

Toe Smear (heel pivot)

Smear

To do a **smear**, apply appropriate **footweighting** (▽, above: pivot on toe to smear heel) and **torque** the foot in the **desired arc** (below). You **torque** the foot (feet) by ① **foot twist** (least effective), ② **leg twist/knee swing**, or ③ **whole body torque** (tricky but most effective)

① ② ③

Ⓐ upper body torques to the left...

Ⓑ ...which twists the legs to the left

Excepting crossover and pivot **turns**, __all__ turns are smeared turns.!. For example, tilt your skates left and, _if_ they're heel-weighted, the skates go to the left doing a toe smear.

Ⓒ ...which smears the toes of the skates to the left.

Elementary Smeared Turns...

A-line Turns are extended smears done by alternating foot weighting. To turn right you weight your left skate, Ⓐ. Since it's on the inside edge, it will track right when weighted. As you turn to the right you're heel smearing: pivoting the skates on the ground, creating the turn arc, Ⓑ

The same smear that causes the right turn also functions as a brake because of wheel edge friction, working at an angle to your original direction

This is why beginners are taught the A-line Turn & Brake first; your constantly smearing skates keep your speed low and control high!

As your A-line turn skills improve you'll notice individual elements comprising the A-line Turn: ① Knee in/knee out which rotates the feet inside/outside, ② Skate "Tilt" which controls how much edge you've using (direction & speed control), ③ "Smearing torque" (speed control), and ④ "weight shifts" which determine which skate edge establishes the turn direction. The striped arrow shows leg tension which helps establish the turn radius (also a pretty good shock absorber and speed governor used correctly).

Detail

Vector →

Advanced Smearing...

From a parallel stance, you can rotate your knees in concert ("knee swings") right and left to put turning torque on your skates. This knee "input" puts your skates on "turning edges"* and causes micro-smears as the skates rotate from side to side. The smear friction governs your overall speed which is good if you want to go slower overall. To lose less overall speed unweight the "outside" skate, cutting smear friction by 50%!

Fall Line

Linked Knee Swing Parallel Turns

Knee Out (right skate shown)

"Smear"

Vector

Knee Rotated In

"Smear"

Vector

Advanced Toe Pivot Heel Smear Hockey Stop

This is an advanced skill for armored skaters on "hard" durometer wheels! Shift your weight over your toes as you turn. The key to survival is dyno-relaxing your legs, bending knees deeply & bleeding off speed as the heels smear to the outside.

Danger! Example ONLY!

Vector

Weight & center of gravity over toes; heels slide out.

*Left "turning edges" - left skate on outside edge, rt. skate on inside edge

Braking-

The best way to avoid high-speed wipe-outs is to **always**(!) stay in control of your **VELOCITY**.

Most inline

THUD!

Aiiieeeee!

KA-Whump!

Not Braking

skates come equipped with one of three types of brake systems: ① **Fixed Heel Brakes** ("F.H.B.'s"), ② "active" brakes, or ③ power brakes*

...be cool...
..assume the position....
..tuck my upper torso...

Lower your body

Scissor brake foot forward & tilt onto heel

Scre...eeeech!

Fixed Heel Brake

Fixed Heel Brake:

To operate it you must scissor the braking foot forward semi-unweighted, raise the toe and begin shifting your weight onto the brake heel. Before applying pressure onto the brake do the usual **pre-crash procedure**: ...bend knees, scissor, semi-tuck the upper torso, bring up your hands, put on your helmet (just kidding) & pray... Actually, **F.H.B.'s** work just as good as their operator **is** (you)! If you live in flatland, F.H.B.'s are great! But...if you're learning to skate in a hilly environment, you will probably find that raising your **boot toe to brake** in a critical **high-speed** situation is a **problem**: ① raising the front three wheels reduces the length of your stance, subtracting stability when you need it most! ② going fast with your forefoot on the rearmost wheel can feel **real** squirrelly when you're concentrating on surviving a deteriorating situation (a runaway, for example), ③ Your brain will become **paralyzed** with fear and will **not** allow your leg muscles to **lift** your toe & ground the brake pad..oof! Once you've gotten some experience with them, **F.H.B.'s** are adequate for anything.

* I've **never** even **seen** "power brakes" so we'll just skip 'em, okay?

58

Active Brakes

Most "active" brakes work by allowing the boot cuff (upper) to rotate rearward which pushes the brake pad onto the ground.

① Calf pressure on back of cuff levers the brake down...

② Brake pad hits pavement, brake engaged

To operate an active heel brake, assume "The Position," scissor the braking foot (rt. foot, usually) forward and lever the boot cuff back with **calf pressure rearwards**. Once the brake pad is down, shift more and more body weight onto the brake foot to get more and more **braking power.**

Aiiieee!

...calm down... ..check body position..

...shift more weight onto brake foot... keep knees well bent...

Whew!

scissor brake foot forward

Screeech!

The advantages of active brakes instead of F.H.B.'s for beginner skaters are many;

① All eight wheels stay on the ground: No loss of stability!, ② No heel-wheel mischief, ③ Used properly (above) you **will stop in control** and going in a straight line ...(big confidence booster!).

Active brakes must be well maintained and correctly adjusted to function well. Whether you choose to run F.H.B.'s or active brakes, always replace worn brake pads. If you're running active brakes in hilly areas, carry an extra brake pad and know how to readjust and service the mechanism in the field.

* Rollerblade™ Active Brake Technology (ABT™) system shown. Uh... please don't sue me, dudes!

59

If you use **active brakes**, avoid the tendency to **straighten** the braking leg (after slowing) to rest leg muscles. You'll **lose** significant braking power plus the **ability to absorb shocks**.

‼? oo

o o whew!

Scrrreeech

Thok!

Stiff braking leg

Should your brakes be unable to stop you in time, deep-bend your knees until your non-braking knee contacts the pavement, add weight and you've got a **2nd brake pad**. If that fails, roll to the side and slide. By dipping your knees, half the **fall** is already done...

Not gonna stop before th intersection... !∂✱?!

o o

Screeeeeeeech

deep kneebend

fall & slide

har har har!

So many pedestrians so little time

Detail: kneepad "brake" plus hard calf-lever on braking skate!

Once **beyond** the advanced-intermediate skill level, many skaters remove the entire **brake** apparatus for unencumbered pivots & spins [the brake frame <u>can</u> get in the way sometimes] or to play hockey, etc. If you're a flatlander this is no problem usually, <u>but</u>, if you're a hillbilly like me, you may elect to <u>keep</u> your brake, just in case. Besides, **brakes can fail** so it's good to know how to stop **without brakes**! Next, some proven methods for stopping **sans** brakes...

Elementary Brakeless Stopping...

T-Stop - ① Scissor one skate forward (left, usually) and ② pivot the other foot to the rear ending at a right angle to the lead skate.

③ Using the inside edge of the wheels of the "drag skate", begin applying pressure to the pavement to slow you down. Caution - if you don't apply pressure evenly on all four wheels of the drag foot you'll execute a dynamic spinout (see "toe drag turn", pg. 62 and "toe drag spin", pg 62, too) Finally, to increase your stopping power, shift weight onto the drag skate and tilt it more forward. If you've done the move correctly, you should slide to a stop in a straight line.

"lead skate" ① "drag skate" ②

R+

③ pressure

④

Spinning T-Stop

("Junior Powerslide") - This variation of the normal T-stop (above) involves intentionally doing a controlled 90° spinout at step #2 (above), then powersliding on the "lead skate" (now at a rt. angle to its original position. After you've slowed to almost a com-

Preturn & scissor

1st pivot

weight shift

click!

2nd pivot

smear

weight shift

pivot

yaah!

Turn 90°

Bring feet together

click!

FALL!

plete stop, bring your skates together at a rt. angle to finish. Slow speeds only!! If you attempt this going too fast...wipeout!➔

See "Buttfall" pg 79

61

Toe Drag Brake And Turn

Similar to the standard T-stop except you drag your toe wheel to turn in the **drag direction** ("Toe Drag Turn", left) or to do a gradual slow speed **stop** by applying wheels to the pavement sequentially, toe wheel → heel wheel (Step 2, right) then doing a normal 4 wheel drag as in the T-stop. The key to a smooth stop is smoothly shifting your weight to the "drag skate" (bottom of page)

Turn

rear view

Toe Drag Brake

~~~ **Warning...** ~~~ If you try a toe wheel drag at too high a speed, upon placing the drag skate on the pavement you will be spectacularly spun backwards* and tossed (hopefully) on your butt.   Slow speeds only!

gaaa!   ③   ②   ①

④

Too Fast!

A gradual weight shift onto the "drag skate" during deceleration will prevent a crash 'n burn spin-out (above) if done properly.

heel wheel last   Toe wheel first

Actual Stop   5 mph   10 mph

* Done intentionally, it's a toe drag spin or turn!

62

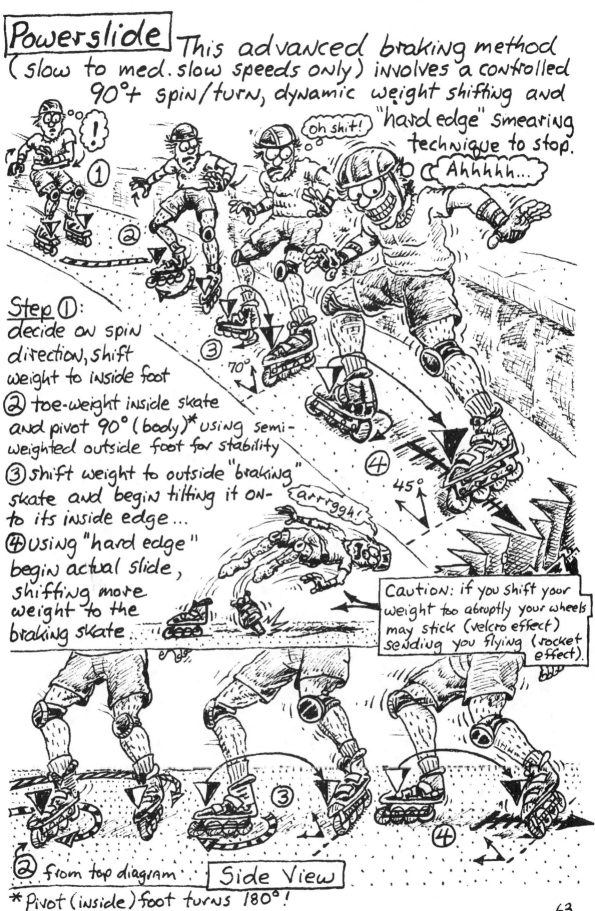

Powerslide

This advanced braking method (slow to med. slow speeds only) involves a controlled 90°+ spin/turn, dynamic weight shifting and "hard edge" smearing technique to stop.

oh shit!

Ahhhhh...

arrrgggh!

Step ①:
decide on spin direction, shift weight to inside foot

② toe-weight inside skate and pivot 90° (body)* using semi-weighted outside foot for stability

③ shift weight to outside "braking" skate and begin tilting it onto its inside edge...

④ using "hard edge" begin actual slide, shifting more weight to the braking skate...

Caution: if you shift your weight too abruptly your wheels may stick (velcro effect) sending you flying (rocket effect).

70°

45°

② from top diagram   Side View

* Pivot (inside) foot turns 180°!

63

Advanced Brakeless Stopping...

You can combine a pivot turn with **wheel edge friction** to do a

Backwards Pivot Stop [low speeds only!]

"T-stop"

VECTOR

Stop at 90° to your vector

Forward scissor the leg on the side you'd like to turn 30°-90°...①, (left leg forward, turn left, etc).

② Preturn the upper torso and

③ Tilt (slightly) up onto both toe wheels [½"-2"] and continue the torso twist. You <u>should</u> execute a near right-angle turn (or fall on your ass!) and end up backward, perpendicular to your original vector. Bend your knees deeper to absorb momentum ④ and bring your "inside" skate heel into the instep of the "outside" skate. This should bring you to a snappy stop, if you bled off enough speed! Wear your butt-armor.

180° Backwards Pivot Stop

After you've mastered the above pivot move, try pivoting 180° instead of 90° (steps ① & ② stay the same). Add a <u>little</u> speed to the twist on your toes to do a full 180°. Do <u>not</u> over-torque on the pivot... this is a fluid move using minimal body-english*, ② left. Once you're skating backwards, weight the "outside skate and smear on a well-bent knee as you "carve" a 90° turn, ④. The weight shift from inside to outside skate should be gradual to allow the outside skate to sweep and smear with its inside edges. When you've bled off enough speed, bring the skates together heel to instep for a perfect T-stop (you hope!)

*"minimal" is the least possible effort to execute the move.

64

Before you seriously attempt any moves like "backwards pivot stops", you may want to learn actual → | Backwards Skating | Find a very clean,* smooth, flat (or very slightly inclined) piece of pavement. Begin with a backwards swizzle and gradually narrow your stance until your feet are parallel & shoulder-wide. Concentrate your weight just forward of the center of your skates... try to apply wide and even foot pressure in the boot to swallow little bumps, etc. Use short, grounded outstrokes with as much glide as possible. Skating backwards requires not only a mental "move" reversal (forward to backward)...

Swizzle Technique

...you've also got a big fat blind spot to deal with! [see "Doing the Linda Blair", pg. 29] To turn, add weight to the foot opposite the desired turn direction ("O.D.F.") and let your body follow the turning skate. As your technique improves the weighted-foot turn becomes a cut turn, adding power and smear friction (if needed). I recommend that beginners NOT try backwards skating without ① butt armor, ② solid backwards A-Line and swizzle skills, and ③ a generally good beginner skill repetoire.

Parallel Technique

!*D?*!

*Hitting even a pea-size pebble can get you hurt when skating backwards! See "Butt Armor", pg 7

Blind Spot

Backward Skating For Beginners

Backwards Swizzle

Outstroke · Instroke · Instroke · Outstroke

Apex

Backward swizzling is definately the **best** way to learn to skate backwards; ...you've got huge inside-edge wheel contact (friction/speed control) plus excellent stability 'cause you're in a modified **A-Line** stance. You also get a free "foot-weighting" lesson; to keep from falling on your face (toe-weighting) you'll learn to apply your weight just forward of center. Don't forget to keep your knees bent, even at the apex of the out-stroke! Once you're feeling relatively solid swizzling **straight** backwards, try "hard-weighting" each skate successively to do **linked turns!** Hard-weighting plus outstroking will give you a feel for "**cuts**": sort of a half a backward swizzle — only one skate outstrokes in a sweeping motion, the other (inside) skate "follows" the dominant outstroking skate. (Next page).

CUT · CUT · CUT

Learning to "cut" your skates going backward gives you a skill foundation for mastering moves like backwards crossunders, reverse spins, etc.

Linked Turns and "Cut" Strokes

Another excellent technique for **backwards skating** is using "cuts": sweeping outstrokes ("outside" foot") using "hard weighting" on the **inside edge** of the cutting skate.

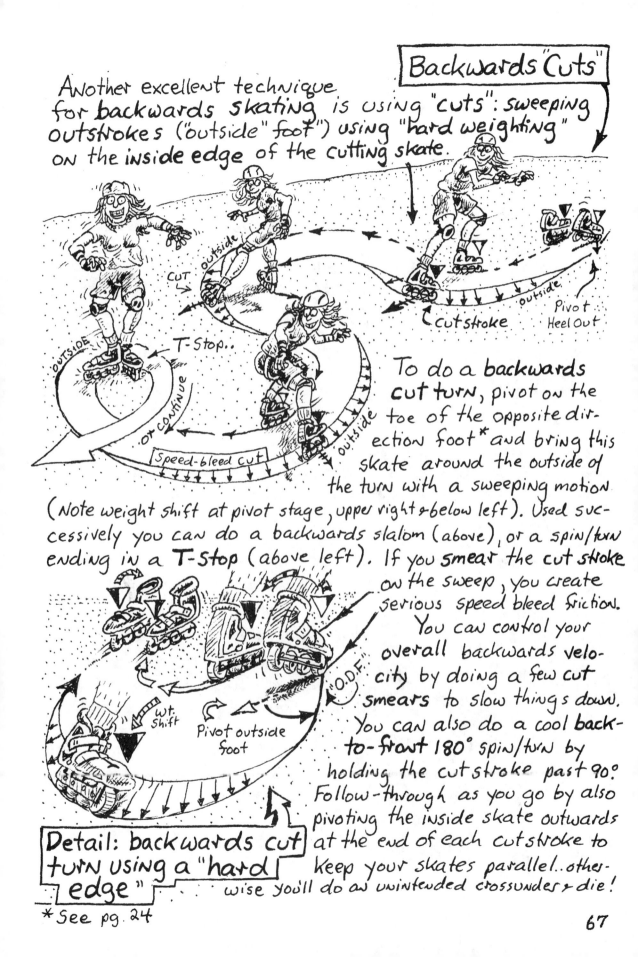

CUT

outside

outside

cutstroke

outside

Pivot Heel Out

OUTSIDE

OUTSIDE

T-Stop..

or continue

Speed-bleed cut

outside

To do a **backwards cut turn**, pivot on the toe of the opposite direction foot* and bring this skate around the outside of the turn with a sweeping motion (Note weight shift at pivot stage, upper right & below left). Used successively you can do a backwards slalom (above), or a spin/turn ending in a **T-Stop** (above left). If you **smear** the cut stroke on the sweep, you create serious speed bleed friction.

You can control your overall backwards velocity by doing a few cut smears to slow things down. You can also do a cool **back-to-front 180° spin/turn** by holding the cut stroke past 90°. Follow-through as you go by also pivoting the inside skate outwards at the end of each cut stroke to keep your skates parallel..otherwise you'll do an unintended crossunder & die!

"O.D.F."

wt. shift

Pivot outside foot

Detail: backwards cut turn using a "hard edge"

* See pg. 24

By now you're semi-familiar **Learning Curve** with the rudiments of inline skating; A-Line, Swizzle, Basic stroke, Backward skating, simple turns, braking, etc. At some point you've gotten a little **road rash*** and hit the pavement a few times...sometimes you seem to be **UNLEARNING** even the simplest moves. This is known as falling off the **learning curve**...

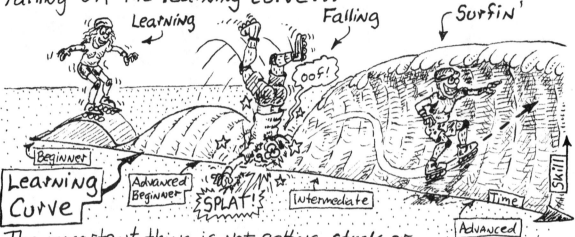

Learning   Falling   Surfin'

oof!

Beginner

Learning Curve

Advanced Beginner

SPLAT!

Intermediate

Time

Skill

Advanced

The important thing is not getting **stuck** or excessively **freaked** out by falls and learning setbacks. A lot of falls & slips usually means you're needing to go back a few steps and progress a little more slowly. If you're skating on the top edge of the learning curve, occasional falls are **normal**; you're challenging yourself **appropriately** and a slump in learning every once in a while is natural. To learn new stuff &

Zen Learning Experience...

Tha-Wap!

Thank you, master...

improve old skills, you have to find **a balance point** between challenging yourself (some falls) and over-reaching yourself (a **lot** of falls). Once you find your personal balance point you'll be working at the "edge" and surfing the **Learning Curve!**

*   ouch ouch ouch   **Road Rash**

youch!

68

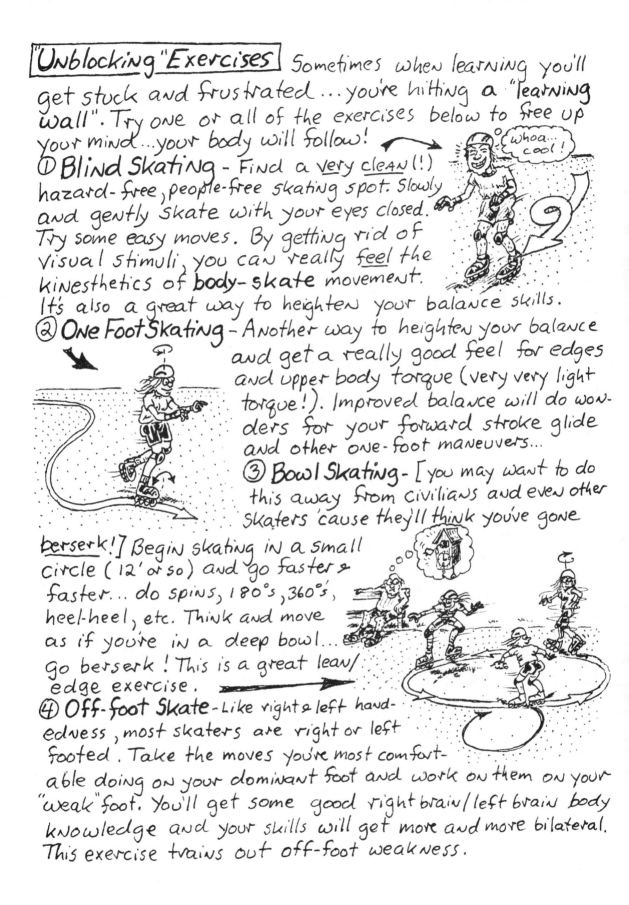

"Unblocking" Exercises Sometimes when learning you'll get stuck and frustrated...you're hitting a "learning wall". Try one or all of the exercises below to free up your mind...your body will follow!

① Blind Skating - Find a very clean (!) hazard-free, people-free skating spot. Slowly and gently skate with your eyes closed. Try some easy moves. By getting rid of visual stimuli, you can really feel the kinesthetics of body-skate movement. It's also a great way to heighten your balance skills.

whoa... cool!

② One Foot Skating - Another way to heighten your balance and get a really good feel for edges and upper body torque (very very light torque!). Improved balance will do wonders for your forward stroke glide and other one-foot maneuvers...

③ Bowl Skating - [you may want to do this away from civilians and even other skaters 'cause they'll think you've gone berserk!] Begin skating in a small circle (12' or so) and go faster & faster... do spins, 180°s, 360°s, heel-heel, etc. Think and move as if you're in a deep bowl... go berserk! This is a great lean/edge exercise.

④ Off-foot Skate - Like right & left handedness, most skaters are right or left footed. Take the moves you're most comfortable doing on your dominant foot and work on them on your "weak" foot. You'll get some good right brain/left brain body knowledge and your skills will get more and more bilateral. This exercise trains out off-foot weakness.

"Cutting out"
with a Mohawk
Spin
(see pg. 112)

Falling

So face it, you're going to fall, probably a _lot_! It's your **karmic debt** for all of the ecstatic FUN you will have when you begin skating _without falling_, which, believe it or not, will happen eventually! For your first 40 hours of actual skating, wear too much armor: wristbrace, knee & elbow pads, butt armor and a helmet, always! Try to turn ass-over-elbow death falls into semi-controlled falls whenever possible. With the exception of an actual face-plant, _all_ the following fall types can be used as emergency braking methods and bailouts under the life-threatening circumstances we often get ourselves into...

Classic "Frontal Fall"

also "Full Facial", "Face Grind", "Face-plant", "Lip Brakes", "Header" - Usually caused by front wheels hitting a bump, edge, or pavement irregularity, undercutting the skater and causing a face-plant or headfirst baseball slide. Avoid by center-weighting feet & keeping knees bent to absorb bumps & shocks.

Yiiieee!

oof!

Face Plant

Obstacle Undercut

Head-first Baseball Slide*: ground contact sequence; ① hand heels, ② elbows, ③ knees, & ④ toes

yeek!

Thock!

① ② ③ ④

*Note: A true "master-slider" can do this slide on just his/her toe-wheels and wrist pads!

73

Basic Controlled Frontal Fall

Begin to **control** your fall <u>before</u> you're totally out of control! The moment you sense an impending fall ("decision horizon"), immediately **take action** to regain some control before it's too late!

Assume "The Position" (①), Lower your torso (②), drop to your (padded) knees (③). Continue falling forward onto <u>heels</u> of hands and elbows (<u>if</u> padded)(④), and hopefully slide to a stop (⑤). Follow through (optional): drop a shoulder and somersault into an upright crouch, skates perpendicular to the fall line (below).

② Lower your body...

③ Drop to your knees...

④ Apply hand heels and elbows (if padded) to pavement...

⑤ Finish sliding on hands, knees and toes...

Follow Through (optional)

Fall Line

Use the last of the deceleration energy to roll heels-overhead into an upright crouching stance. This semi-judo rolling flip spreads out the energy of the fall and ends in a favorable body position (upright!) and gives flash to a very un-flashy situation.

74

Sideways Fall- One of the "better" ways to fall. Go with it and try to resist the urge to put out a hand to catch the fall...you're risking a busted wrist...

yow!

Tuck & Roll

...if you do, especially at speed. Tuck and roll to dis-sipate fall energy and bleed off speed. If you're wearing your pads you should come through the fall fairly intact!

Awk!

THUD!

OOF!

yiieee!

Backwards Fall [see "Buttfall," pg. 79]
Potentially the most injurious of the "routine" falls; there is no way to pre-fall (collapse your body position) or to safely roll out of it. Basically your feet go up in the air and you land full force on your butt (bad!) or your back (worse) and/or on the back of your head and neck (really bad!!). Pads help but it's better to learn to avoid backwards falls altogether; first assume "The Position" and imagine some heavy duty chains running from your waist to your ankles that prevent straight-ening your legs at all. This keeps your weight over your toes. Also imagine more shackles running from knees to elbows that keep your upper torso bent forward and your hands in the "sight picture".

Kinky!

Buttfall Chastity Belt

Bailing Out and a Few More Interesting Ways to Stop...

Stylin' Grass Dive- "Stale Japan" Grounder

Swoosh

When learning about hills, velocity & traffic as a novice, sometimes it is prudent to grass dive or otherwise punch-out <u>before</u> you completely lose control & get dinged in a really major way...

merde!

AWK!

Rolling *Grass Stop & minor curb hop: low to medium speeds

High-speed Grass Dive (standard "Front Fall" protocol)

*Be prepared to fall forward if your wheels bog down!

Bailing Out By Falling...

Although it is (believe it or not) much more difficult to **intentionally** fall **rearward** into a feet-first **baseball slide** than it is to fall forward into the standard hands-and-knees "**braking fall**", sometimes it is more advantageous to risk your **ass** literally to avoid the possibility of **head** and **neck** injuries...

Intentional Buttfall

Boom!

damn!

puta!

① Decide to try a baseball slide feet-first...

② Deep knee-bend and semi-tuck...

oof!

③ Roll back onto your butt and lay out to brake with body, feet in the air...(youch!)

KA-BOOM!

④ Strike obstacle feet first and, hopefully, skate away unhurt...

har har!

Avoiding Buttfalls...

Dumbass!

Lookit all thoses pads... **WIMP!**

Har har!

CLACK!

Actual True story

So, after a whole bunch of buttfalls and forward falls, etc. you eventually learn ① to keep your knees bent (!!) and ② to keep your weight over the front third of the skate (toe area), and ③ to wear appropriate protective gear. You will also learn that backward falls are the absolute worst kind of fall; you can't control the energy (vs. "hand-elbow-knee-toe" frontfall energy dissipation) and it's real easy to bust a wrist and/or elbow attempting to check the fall.

Experiment as much as you can tolerate on dirt or grass...you'll discover that if your knees are bent & your toes are weighted, you have to **work** to fall backwards!

Ulp! Not again!

FOOM!

Appropriate buttwear

Falling

Not Falling

Other Unconventional Stopping Methods...

Warning! These are desperate moves for desperate situations!

You can grab a sign post and spin around it to **decelerate** or to change your vector...

Aiiieeeee!

VINE

OW!

New Vectors

If grass diving isn't an option and you've got to get on the ground quickly (without knocking out your teeth on a frontal fall), try a **toe drag spin** to initiate a **rolling tumble.**

scheit!

!

ACME moving

Phew!

THUD!

huh!?

Bailing Out

Never grab another skater to stop or steady yourself!

① ♫♪

yiiieeeee

② Thud

③ Nice tackle, butt-munch!

Uhh... Sorry

While pedestrians may be considered **fair game** in a survival situation, grabbing another skater to check a fall or a runaway is absolutely **not done** (!) without the express **consent** of the grabee.

④ NO! NO! NO!

Ow! Ek! Yow!

If an **experienced** skater so **chooses**, he/she can contact the out-of-control skater and assist in the recovery. Or, in worst case scenarios, simply **body-check** the **geek** into the grass, mosh-style!

Yeek!

Yo! Grab my Arm...

Screeeech

Errr... Thanks!

Anytime Bro!

If you're really serious about being a total **pinhead**, there are many **soft targets** to choose from in the **urban environment...**

Meals On Wheels!

Intermediate
To
Advanced
Skills...

gaaa!

Now I **know** enough to **really** get hurt!!

☆Intermediate☆

So, hopefully you survived the beginner/novice stage without too much brain and/or body damage... you can skate forward and backward (a little), stop, turn, etc. etc.. Going upward and onward from the novice level is **mostly** a matter of putting a lot of miles on your skates, expanding on the techniques you already know, and learning from other skaters via the age-old process of "hangin' out and **mucking around on skates**". The following 6 pages are an outline for learning plus some additional skills & tips needed on the **intermediate** path, followed by detailed drawings of **some** of the more complex moves. Many of these skills have been covered in the beginner section and your job is mastering & polishing them in order to become a solid intermediate skater. Remember- this is only **one path** among many leading to your becoming an **advanced recreational street skater**. Most skaters are hardcore individualists and it is guaranteed that your goals, learning speed, and physical abilities will be way different from mine! Perhaps by studying my **thrash-and-burn** experiences you'll avoid serious injury and maybe even find a short-cut on the rocky path to True Inline Skating Enlightenment!

we hiked all the way up here for **that**!?

Uh.. let's see... "stroke like the antelope in tall grass, glide like the flight of the lonely peregrine..."

what!

Er...does anybody have a 5/32 allen wrench?

Most intermediate skills are a continuum of the skills you learned as a beginner. Just add lots of practice, polish, and skating experience to work your way up the skill ladder. Refer to the Beginner section for step by step technical details.

① Begin to add upper-body torque to your spins and turns for power and flash... ⇨

①

②

Torque your forward stroke too!

② Endeavor to become more & more comfortable skating in the third dimension... air!

③ Learn to skate in arcs, curves and circles instead of straight lines...

④ The width of your cruising stance will decrease as you improve overall. Scissoring for a long stance at speed becomes instinctual...

Narrower stance

well-scissored

⑤ Broaden your terrain horizon by shifting from flatland to hills and other dynamic features whenever possible *...

WOOSH!

yay-ha!

*or whenever it would be amusing...

85

⑥ Learn **economy of movement**... which means you learn to subtract **unnecessary** movements and, where desired, add flash to tart things up. Uneconomical flailing movement ("Thrashin'", rt.) is the opposite of "stylin" (upper rt.)

Stylin'!

Thrashin'

huff. puff. gasp!

⑦ Find a ramp and learn some basic "vert" moves; it'll make you a better skater and teach you basic "move sequencing*.

Aiiieee!

har har

ramp "bacon in the pan."

well... that's what NOT to do...

*move sequencing is basically breaking down a move or trick into component parts in the hopes of learning a hard move in little steps...

⑧ Try to "dress for success"- ie- wear terrain/environment appropriate body Armor...

Just right!

FOOM!

Too little Armor

Too Much Armor

Yo, homeboys! Mind if I bust some moves with your **posse**?

⑨ Check out **skater culture** and maybe learn a little of the language! [see "Glossary"]

"Homeboys"!

uhh.... **No!**

..but couldja buy us some beers?

⑩ As you begin to skate on **steeper terrain**, to survive the experience you'll need to quickly develop some advanced high-speed braking and **evasion** techniques...

① Lamp-post swing

② car vault

MAIN PINE

AAARGH!!

⑪ Learn to skate well on **one foot**! This will do wonders for your ~~forward~~ **stride**, **turns**, and **spins**. Try to practice equally on your right and left foot * so you don't develop a "**weak side**" on the un-practiced foot.

* bilateral practice

← Good for learning about edges too...

⑫ Work on your backwards skating 'til you're doing comfortable "180° Front To Back" demi-spins at low to medium speeds...

yeah!

↑ 180° Front To Back

↑ 180° Back To Front

↑ 180° Back To Front

...also learn the exit move, a "180° Back To Front" spin.
These two moves are your key to flashier advanced spins & spin stops.

⑬ Add "commitment" to your turns and spins by using hard edges and dynamic weight shifts; you want to make the move happen, not just let it happen. (passive vs. aggressive move)

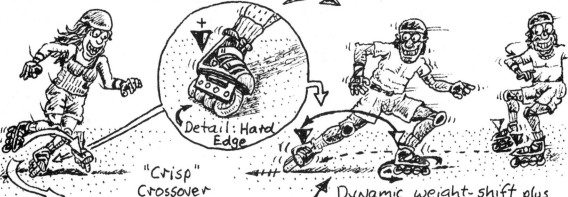

Detail: Hard Edge

"Crisp" Crossover Turn
[understroke & stepover]

Dynamic weight-shift plus a hard edge, the last move of the powerslide.

Decelerating Turn - Actively bleeding speed via edge friction while parallel (non-crossover) turning. The harder the edge the lower the speed!

⑭ As you begin skating on many **different surface types**, familiarize yourself with all the **different handling characteristics** you experience: brick walks, new asphalt, old asphalt, grooved & smooth concrete, "mafia concrete" * hard-packed dirt, etc, etc. Knowing the **feel** of different surfaces will help your street skating **flow**. Also you can easily car-scout new routes and loops **before** committing yourself to ten miles of pebbly, decrepit asphalt HELL!

Old fissured & patched Asphalt

New Asphalt "black ice"

"mafia" Concrete

Eeech!

⑮ High-speed **night skating is loads of fun** and, if you **survive**, will really improve your reaction time and **dynamic** (seat-of-the-pants) **style!** Also, far fewer civilians will see you if you take a fall...

woo!

damn!

⑯ **Practice** dealing with real street hazards (grates, curbs, cracks, crack vials, etc.) so you'll have an experiential foundation for dealing with them "at speed" on unfamiliar terrain. Also experiment with **wheel cohesion / body lean** on **wet** or **dewy** road surfaces.

Diagonalizing a grate to avoid trapping a wheel...

You'll be amazed how easily damp pavement can woof you!

* concrete that has crumbled while relatively young...

And NOW, some actual NEW skills...

Introduction to Bumps, Drops And "Air"

Whether or not you actually **want** to skate over bumps and off drops, **if you skate on the street, you will do bumps and drops!** Since it's always preferable to do the really tricky stuff intentionally & under semi-controlled conditions, here are a few ways to aggressively habituate yourself to **gnarly** street conditions...

Once you've mastered a small drop, instead of going to a bigger drop, try the small one **again**; faster, backward, one-footed, etc. The main thing is to learn to react correctly and instinctively to a **stream of mixed surfaces, drops, and bumps** so that, when you're skating unfamiliar ground, you won't fall and bust your **ass!**

91

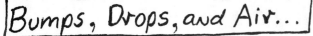

Bumps, Drops, and Air...

Another good reason to **repeat familiar drops** is to develop a feel for the fine points of precision "foot **weighting**": toe weighting, ball-of-foot weighting, midfoot weighting, etc. You will definately learn to **avoid** heel wheel landings* or any landings with your center of gravity behind the "Midfoot Balance Point." (see "Buttfalls," pg 79)

*Unless you're intentionally doing drops **backwards**!

Aerial Body Movement

Freeze Frame (Static)
vs.
Dynamic Jumps...

"Freeze"

Body quiet above knees

Set Landing Stance

CLOP!

Freeze Frame (Static) - The safest mode of aerial movement is NONE at all! In freeze frame style jumping you set your landing stance before takeoff. This way, by minimalizing airborne movement, you limit the opportunities to totally screw up the jump. (also known as "quiet body")

Dynamic Jump This is essentially adding flashy movement during the jump. Looks great done well but if you don't land with skates parallel to the jump vector you'll execute a very colorful body grind...yow!

Yeeek

oof!

Ka-Klunk!

Learn to do static jumps <u>first</u>. Once you've very solid doing small air, you can safely begin adding small moves incrementally. Proceed slowly, concentrating on reverse move sequencing; doing air moves (even small ones) requires building the move sequence <u>backward</u> from the landing stance! Landing in control is the prime directive when working on air moves!

LANDING STANCE

4,3,2,1

Err Forward...

When playing around on ramps and drops, concentrate on landing with your weight over the balls of your feet. If your weight is too far forward, you'll do a dynamic "superman slide", which is a much more controlled falling technique than falling backwards!

darn

ACH!

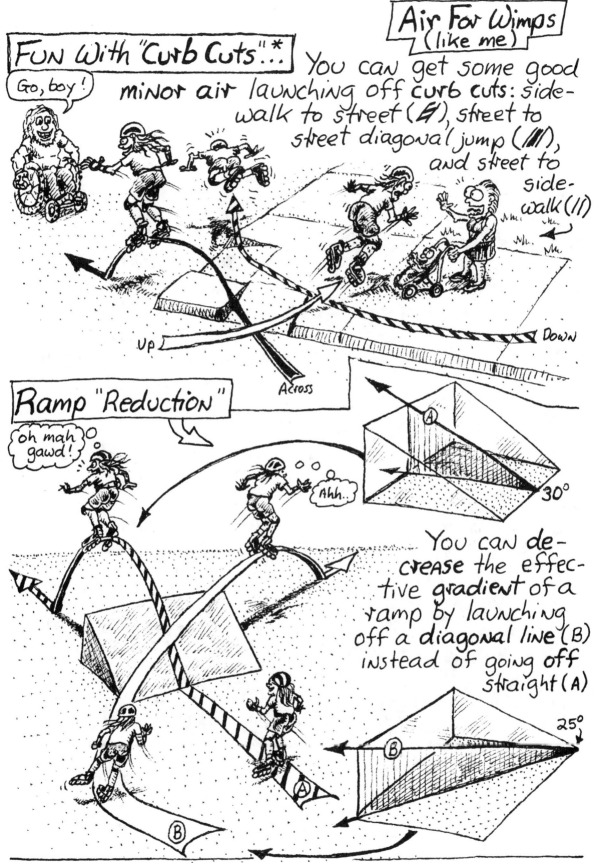

FUN With "Curb Cuts"...*

Go, boy!

Air For Wimps (like me) You can get some good minor air launching off curb cuts: side-walk to street (≡), street to street diagonal jump (///), and street to side-walk (//)

Up

Across

Down

Ramp "Reduction"

oh mah gawd!

Ahh...

A

30°

You can de-crease the effec-tive gradient of a ramp by launching off a diagonal line (B) instead of going off straight (A)

B

25°

A

B

* small ramps that allow wheelchair access to street/sidewalk

95

Amping A Ramp

side view

waaahhh!

③

④

oof!

front view

Anti-swallow

② ①

Or "How to make a **simple ramp launch** into a **fearsome** thing to behold"...

① lower (coil) your body to a **near-squat** at the top of the ramp, ② spring upwardly as you hit the **lip**, ③ **flap** your arms furiously to avoid losing it and doing a ④ face-first **swan dive!**

"Swallowing" A Ramp

A very useful skill to know when you suddenly **wuss out** halfway up a ramp (or jump)...

① relax your legs and let the ramp's up energy* coil your body, then ② lower your legs

urk!

too fast... shit!

①

1. See pg. 98 [* "lift"]

Stepovers

You can avoid doing an awkward series of hops when skating across bad sections of pavement by doing some fancy footwork. "Stepovers", a combination of running strides, allow you to move smoothly over cracks, joints, potholes and such.

Doing high-speed stepovers calls for quick and precise weighting/unweighting of alternating skates.

STEPOVERS

Done at speed, this can be the ultimate in seat-of-your-pants "reaction" street skating. Fully mastered, good stepover technique is a great street survival skill but expect to take some pretty good falls in the learning stages. In other words, wear lots of armor and practice a lot...

boing! boing! shit!

'scuse me sir... how do I get to Lincoln Center?

Practice Practice Practice.

From our "New Uses For Lame Old Jokes" Dept.

Hops and Swallows...

Swallow
(level)

Swallow
(down)

CLOP!

Ⓐ

Lots of
smaller obstacles
(cracks, bumps, etc.)
can be hopped over or rolled over
on unweighted skates (level swallow, above left).
Basically you do a swallow by allowing your body
(mainly legs) to flex deeply to Ⓐ absorb shock going
off a drop (above rt.) or Ⓑ pull upwards to clear a medium
drop-off (1'-3') by bringing Swallow (up)   flex

your feet up to the
lip of the drop-off
without actually "hop-
ping". Your head
should stay level
pretty much until
you unflex your body
after you've cleared
the edge of the
drop.

Head Level

2' drop

unflex

Ⓑ

Hopping In Detail...

Like doing air moves, hopping is an "active" technique. You're not merely absorbing shock, you're coiling your body and springing from point A to point B.

① Lock eyes on drop or obstacle...
② Coil body...
③ Uncoil body (spring up)
④ raise feet additionally for extra clearance (optional)..
⑤ swallow the landing shock (optional)..
and ⑥ return to upright position.

Point B

Point A

The length of the hop is determined by your forward speed; going 2 mph you travel a couple feet in the air. Going 20 mph you travel almost 20 feet on the same hop height! [obviously, we're talkin' a big hop]

Even though at slow speeds you travel only a few feet horizonally, you can squeeze in a little extra distance once you've touched down by doing a swallow just before landing. This keeps your skates unweighted a few nano-seconds longer, even though the wheels are on the ground. This little extra "travel" can become very significant if you've missed your mark and don't want to do a face-plant!

Doing a well-timed emergency swallow can keep you upright and rolling even if your wheels catch the lip going over!

Hop

hop "travel" w/o swallow

swallow

Hop & swallow

longer hop travel

Descending Stairs You can descend sets of steps by walking down, sliding the handrail,* jumping, or "riding". Stair-riding is bouncing off each step & swallowing as much shock as possible. It's not steepness but tread width that determines the doability of a staircase; if the tread of the steps is wider than the length of your skate, it's ok. If the tread is only as wide or less than your skate length, walk it or jump it! →

hot damn! I'm good!

Ride Jump CLOP!

Tread too Narrow

45°

Rise = Run · too steep!

Tread "rise"
←"run"→ ↑"rise"
Tread
↑"rise" "steepness"
detail

steepness acceptable

!Caution (again)! ↘

Tread width OK

When doing jumps, remember that an airborne skate will follow the first wheel(s) to hit the ground. Skating (flying) forward, a toe-wheel landing tracks straight; a heel wheel landing causes a wild-ass pivot that'll put your buttocks on the pavement double quick! Weight forward!

② ①

weight

Aiiieee!

Toe Landing

Heel Landing

*See "wüss railslide, p. 146!

100

Speaking of going **down** things, it's time to...

Get Comfortable With Hills...

Learning how to deal with serious inclines and very high speeds requires a stratagizing and incremental "conservative" approach. Also learn to relax (to be physically loose and mentally at ease) and have _fun_! First find a long slight incline ("hill") with a good runout, lots of bailout possibilities, free of debris, traffic, etc.

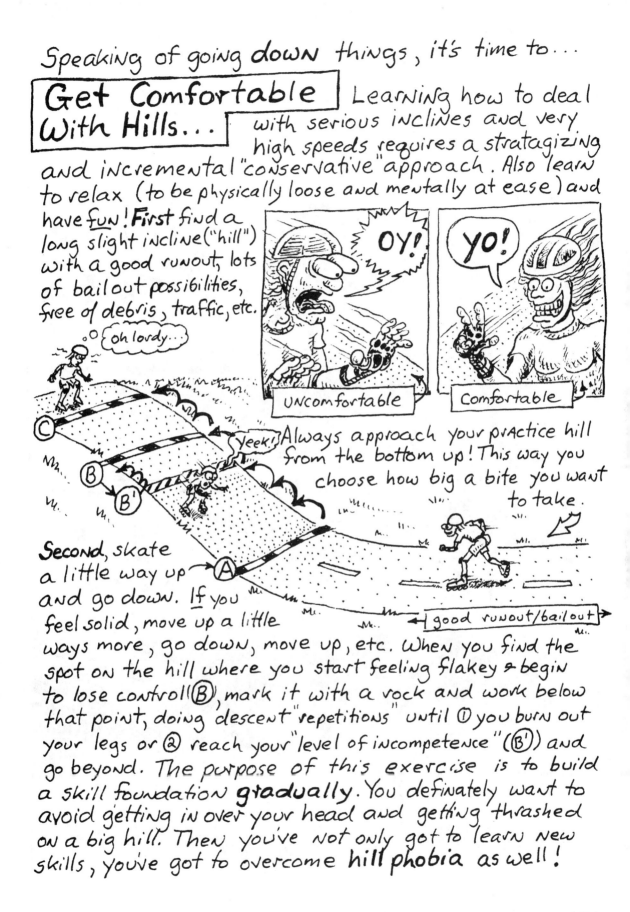

oh lordy...

OY!

YO!

UNcomfortable

Comfortable

Yeek!

Always approach your practice hill from the bottom up! This way you choose how big a bite you want to take.

Second, skate a little way up and go down. If you feel solid, move up a little

good runout/bailout

ways more, go down, move up, etc. When you find the spot on the hill where you start feeling flakey & begin to lose control Ⓑ, mark it with a rock and work below that point, doing descent "repetitions" until ① you burn out your legs or ② reach your "level of incompetence" (Ⓑ¹) and go beyond. The purpose of this exercise is to build a skill foundation **gradually**. You definately want to avoid getting in over your head and getting thrashed on a big hill. Then you've not only got to learn new skills, you've got to overcome **hill phobia** as well!

Pre-scouting Hills

How to choose *downhill* runs:
(A) gradient- steep but doable...
(B) hazards - few, intersection..
(C) bail out spots - tons!
(D) traffic - thin, good
runout past hill...
(see rt. →)

ulp!

?

Excellent Run-
out: plenty of stopping distance before intersection
and small uphill stretch
for brakeless
deceleration..
M.

STOP

Good Hill

(A) Gradient- too *G!D* steep!
(B) hazards - road debris, etc.
(C) bailout - NO, sorry...
(D) traffic - big time...
runout- NONE whatsoever.

holy
crap!

BAD Hill

Safely Descending Hills: Avoiding Runaways

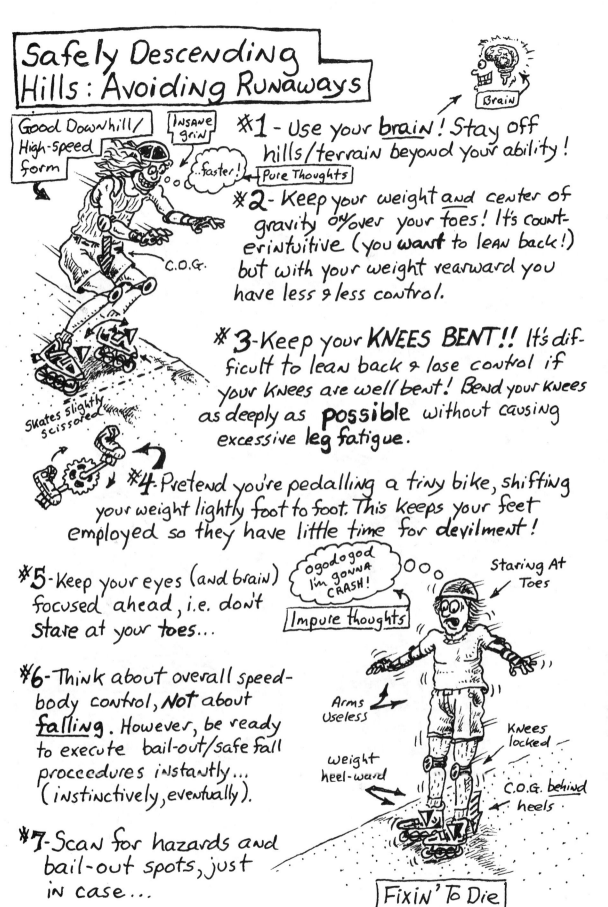

Brain

Good Downhill/High-speed form

Insane grin

..faster!

Pure Thoughts

C.O.G.

Skates slightly scissored

#1 - Use your **brain**! Stay off hills/terrain beyond your ability!

#2 - Keep your weight and center of gravity on/over your **toes**! It's counterintuitive (you **want** to lean back!) but with your weight rearward you have less & less control.

#3 - Keep your **KNEES BENT!!** It's difficult to lean back & lose control if your knees are well bent! Bend your knees as deeply as **possible** without causing excessive **leg** fatigue.

#4 - Pretend you're pedalling a tiny bike, shifting your weight lightly foot to foot. This keeps your feet employed so they have little time for **devilment**!

#5 - Keep your eyes (and brain) focused ahead, i.e. don't stare at your **toes**...

ogodogod I'm gonna CRASH!

Impure thoughts

Staring At Toes

#6 - Think about overall speed-body control, **Not** about **falling**. However, be ready to execute bail-out/safe fall proceedures instantly... (instinctively, eventually).

Arms Useless

weight heel-ward

Knees locked

C.O.G. behind heels

#7 - Scan for hazards and bail-out spots, just in case...

Fixin' To Die

Once you've worked your way incrementally down the hill (Ⓐ→Ⓑ→Ⓒ) and you're feeling solid from the top, get radical! Stroke fast down the hill ①, giant slalom it ②, crossunder loop it ③, skate it backwards ④. You're building a skill repertoire* and gradually habituating yourself to inclines and speed.

oh my god!

Big Fear

yaay-ha!

Actual Learning Curve

No Fear

Experiment with descending "tucked" (faster) vs. descending upright in an open stance, leaning into the airjet and scooping air (slower). Here you're beginning to familiarize yourself with wind drag and advanced body configurations. Now it's time to find a bigger hill!

* bag of tricks, skill depth

Closed body position

open body pos.

tuck   Air Scoop

Descent Styles

Yike!

Foom

Fall Line

Two Descent Extremes:

Traversing Descent: A-line or parallel style. The skater breaks the hill into sections perpendicular to the Fall Line. Slowest descent possible.

Fall Line Descent: parallel tucked style with skates slightly staggered. This skater depends on a rock-solid stance, obstacle evasion and excellent anticipation and braking skills...

Fall Line

Fastest Possible Descent

105

Summary - Descent Options

① **Sans Skate @ Grass Bailout**-When you've fixin' to run-away jump the curb, remove skates & walk to the bottom of the hill. Safest possible descent style. **Low speed** (duh!)!

② **Monoski Inline**- Skates inline, lots of upper body torque and dynamic weight shifts. You can bleed off speed by tightening turns & increasing wheel friction.* Low to med. speeds.

③ **Basic Runaway** - This is what happens if you wait too long to bailout. To avoid a dyno crash & burn, immediately bend knees <u>low</u>, stagger skates slightly, apply brake and pray the **gravity gods** aren't hungry!

④ **A-line ("Snowplow")** - low to med. speed. **Knees bent**, skates wide apart (slightly staggered, if possible), ankles turned in. You're using **inside edges** to create lots of friction. You can toe-in slightly with lots of leg tension to create angular friction (snowplow). **Don't let your feet come together!** Ouch!!

⑤ **Crossunder Switch Stance** - Medium speed. Here you're controlling speed by large "edge friction" of the underskate coupled with a turning speed bleed* by over-weighting the underskate at and beyond the apex of the turn, smearing downhill.

⑥ **Braking Descent**- Simply stand on your brake going down the hill.

⑦ **Parallel "Giant Slalom"**- medium to high speeds - You break the hill down into wide linked turns using edges and turn energy to absorb and/or release speed. Be careful to stay in "The Position" and be ready to scissor into a **braking** stance if you get going too fast. Combine parallel and crossunder styles if <u>additional **speed bleed** capability is needed.</u>

* Turn Speed Bleed:
The <u>less parallel</u> you are to the Fall Line the slower you go. Most dramatic effect occurs between 45° to 90° to the

fall line.

108

Prescouting Hills - Avoiding Runaways

A "runaway" would be any hyperspeed situation ending (maybe) in a loss of control. This is the physical manifestation of the phrase "his/her reach exceeds his/her grasp!".

You can avoid all hills and go slow at all times (no fun) or you can pre-scout potential skating terrain for:

Ⓐ Gradient (steepness) - Pre-scout hills looking at steepness [a small hill walking can be a BIG hill on skates!] Ⓑ Obstacles & Hazards..

Aiiieeeee!!!

storm drains & grates

potholes & fissures

pebbly road patch

debris

Ⓒ Bailout conditions? grass & dirt (good) vs. concrete & parked cars (bad) etc...

Bored Dogs
heh heh heh...
oh heck!

Bored Teens
har har!
Thonk!

Ⓓ Possible vehicular interactions?
① skating into too much traffic... (uncool)... into no traffic (cool).
② Is there a safe "RUNOUT"? (def: level or uphill stretch of pavement before a hazard)
As a rule, the longer the Runout, the steeper the hill you can safely attempt!

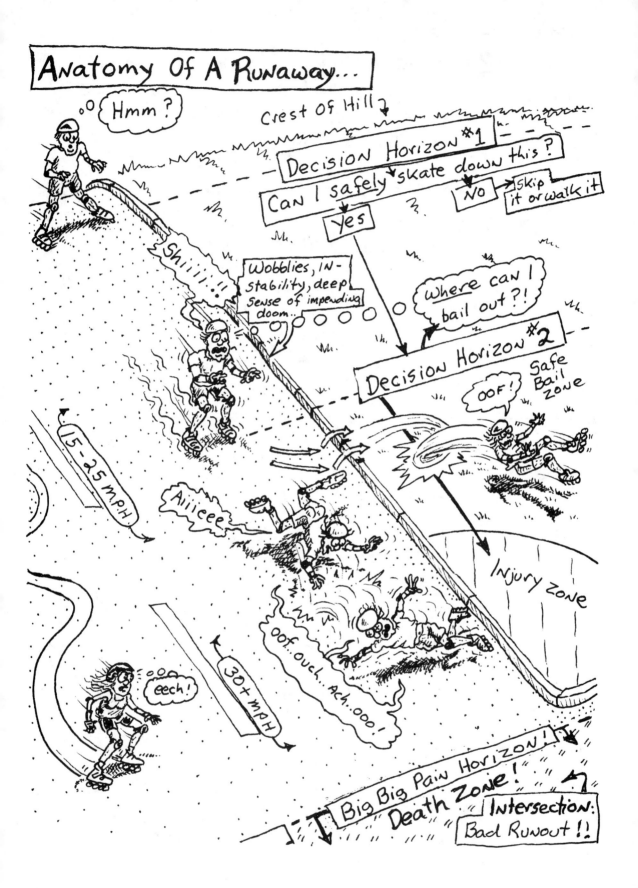

Runaways

¡excremento!

① When a potential runaway is developing, immediately assume the precrash braking stance (brake foot scissored forward, knees well-bent) and attempt to brake and regain control...

② Crouching, scissoring & getting into "The Position" often results in a recovery.. you can keep cruisin', only faster—

③ However, if you're fixing to scream into a busy intersection, desperate measures are appropriate...

?!

Pole Grab

oof!

In other words, when the aircraft catches on fire, BAIL!

Punchin' out!

Thunk!

SUNFF!

holy shi

Aiiieeeee

Soft organic targets are always better than brick walls, autos, trucks, etc.. Lawns, hedges, fat people, large domestic animals, heaps of garbage bags & cardboard boxes make ideal impromtu crash pads!

oh my god!

Body-checking a Hedge

Heel-Heel Braking Spin Also known as the "Mohawk Spin" [see pg. 124] this is a key skill for advanced braking and dynamic concrete surfing!

T-Stop

Heel-Heel Slowing Spin

Rt
Rt

① ② ③ ④ ⑤

Heel-Heel Bailout Spin

In truly desperate situations (no time to brake, no bail zone, etc.) you can initiate a heel-heel spin/turn to bleed off speed and **escape the crash vector** one way or another.
① Preturn & lower your upper torso, shift weight to the "outside" skate, turn "inside" skate 180° and ②...

Awk!

Preturn & weight shift

①

ⓒ
↰
T-Stop

②

Ⓐ "Controlled" Tumble

Yiieee!

Biff!

Ⓑ
"feet-first" belly slide

②Ⓐ "Controlled" Tumble"- tuck & roll & holler!
Ⓑ "feet-first" belly slide - the spin's centrifugal force flings you outside the spin circle and onto the street in (hopefully) the hands 'n knees fall position.. lucky you were wearing your Extreme pads!! Again, at high speeds this is a desperate last-ditch **escape-from-certain-death maneuver!** If you're lucky the move will quickly put you on the pavement in a "controlled" braking slide. If you're truly blessed by the **velocity god** you'll spin upright, bleed speed and ⓒ end with a T-stop (optional) or continue down, slower...

Descending Hills In Control

Below is a summary of slowing/stopping options ranked from beginner to expert (Left to Right) for hills and other high-speed situations...

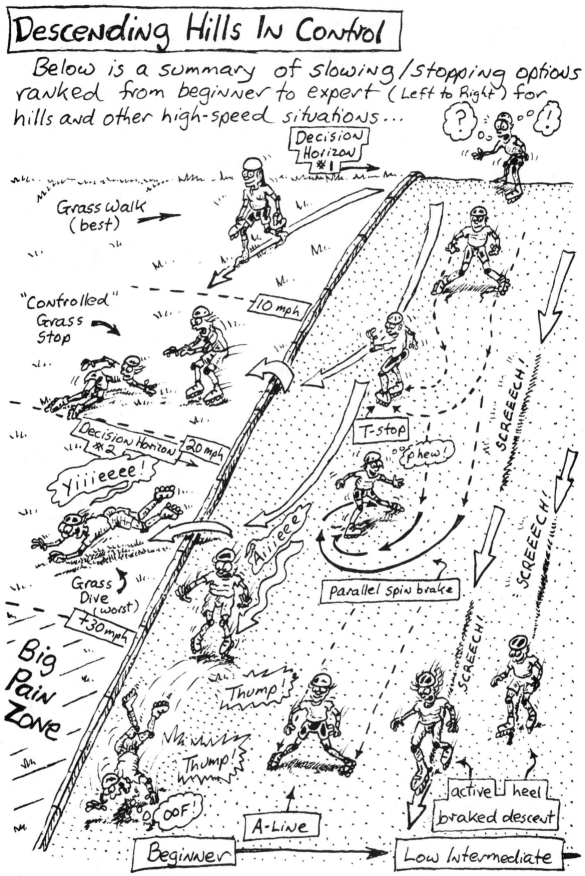

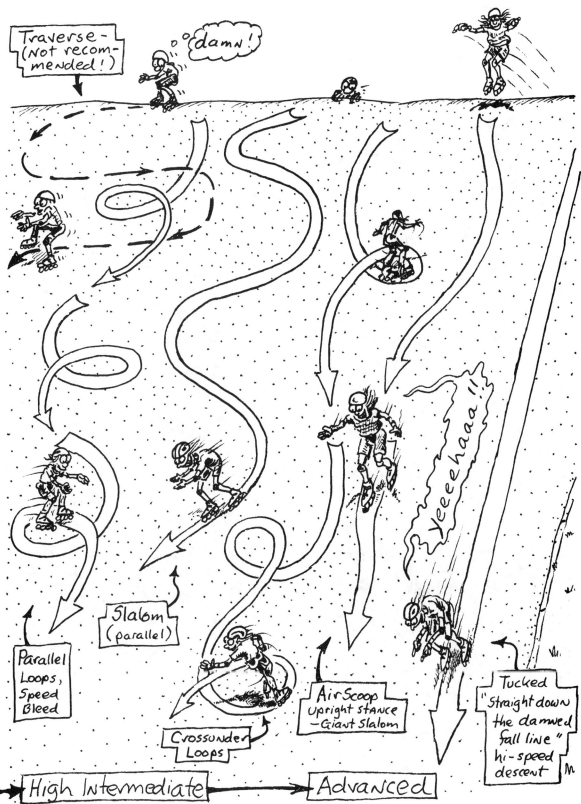

Whenever you're using lots of **edge** you're increasing **friction** which tends to slow you down whether you're "snowplowing" (A-line), crossunder slaloming or parallel slaloming.

A-Line "snowplow"

Crossunder Slalom

Speed Bleed

wind drag

parallel Slalom

Also, you can use a combination of heavy edge pressure and the "airscoop" position (upright, open) as a fairly effective speed "governor" via wind drag plus wheel friction.

Bad Form

Good Form

Long stance

SHORT STANCE

Uneven foot weighting
weight off toes
knees not sufficiently bent

Whatever approach you choose to descend hills always always(!) ① keep your knees well-bent ② keep your legs well-scissored ("long stance") for maximum forward/backward stability ③ keep your weight on the balls of your feet ("toe weighting") for maximum control, and keep weight evenly distributed 50/50 % skate to skate (a wobbly skate at high speed is usually an **UN-weighted skate**!).

Another type of Nasty skate behavior is the "One Foot Wobble", a common downhill problem. Usually it's the "trailing skate" oscillating back and forth which is extremely unnerving at high speeds! If left untreated, the wobble gets worse and worse 'til you lose control and get woofed!

ohmygod I'm gonna diiieeee

yo!

weight uneven!!

reweight

wobblewobblewobble

The **one foot wobble** is almost always caused by having too little weight on the **wobbling skate**. Check your stance (The Position) and reweight your skates 50/50%. Once the offending foot is correctly weighted the wobble will cease!

Remaining **advanced hill techniques** such as **spin stops, spinning speed bleeds**, etc are covered in detail in the "Spins and Turns" section, immediately following.

Pivots, Spins, and Other Demented Behavior...

Spins, pivots and the aerial versions thereof require the highly skillful combination of torque, balance, and coordination (and a wee bit of luck). For people like me, they call for lots of positive body-pavement interaction. But seriously, this is some of the most fun you can have fully-clothed and upright! Be sure to wear your party helmet and lots of body armor when you're attempting this stuff!

Shit! ooo

oof...

WHUMP!

Author's standard Aerial 360..

Ta-dah!

Click!

Heel-Toe 270° Spin/stop

Spin Or Turn?

A "spin" takes place within the vector. The skater's overall direction doesn't necessarily change...

Heel / Heel Spin

Crossover Turn

A "turn" creates a new vector because the skater's overall direction changes

Spins Flat Spin (easiest) ⤵

① ② ③ ④

Begin at **snail** speed, feet shoulder-wide, evenly weighted. Initiate the spin by smoothly twisting the upper torso in the desired spin direction (①). As the lower torso "follows" the twisting upper torso you should execute a 180° to 360° spin (②,③ ④). Keep in mind that this is a gentle finesse move... if you add too much upper torso twist too abruptly, you will **torque** yourself right off your feet! Until you've got it wired, slow & smooth is the key. Add speed & power to the spin by adding **both** forward momentum **and** upper body torque. As you get proficient, notice how your body naturally moves to a heel/toe foot weighting style; the forward-moving (outside) skate becomes the pivot point and the backward-moving (inside) skate merely provides **stability** as you spin.

Basic Spin I

low speed!

Using heel/toe body knowledge from the flat spin, ① raise the heel of the backward-moving "sweep" skate, shift weight to "pivot" skate and turn body into spin cycle.

① Set up

② Spin

Pivot skate

Sweep skate

② Weight the heel of the pivot skate and spin around 180° using "sweep" skate for balance...

③ Center your weight on the pivot skate & bring down the heel of the sweep skate...

③ Follow Through

④ Re-weight feet 50/50

④ Reweight both skates 50/50 & shift foot pressure onto balls of both feet.

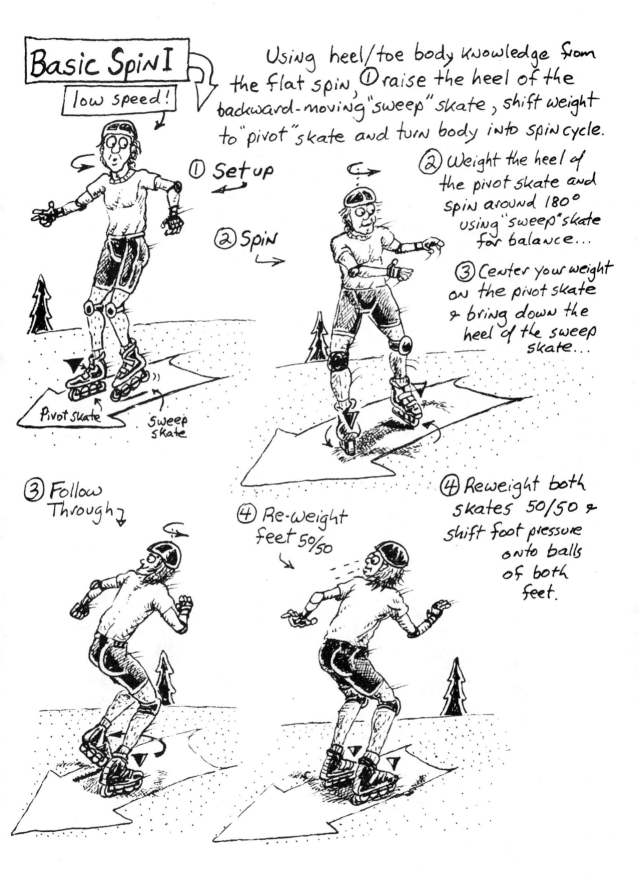

Basic Spin II (advanced)

As you perfect the Flat Spin and Basic Spin I, you'll notice the **body language** is evolving further toward a tight **heel/toe spin**. Now, instead of letting the non-pivot skate sweep wide for stability (below *) keep it under your hips and move weight distribution closer to 50/50...

Basic Spin I

Pivot Skate 90% wt.

* 10% wt.

Sweep Skate, lightly weighted, provides stability during the pivot.

②

Basic Spin II

①

③ Important; minimize upper body torque till you've got the weight shift move wired.

check you later...

HEY!

Basic Spin II, cont'd

more dynamic ("crisp") add forward momentum, not upper body torque...

To make this spin quicker and

Too much upper body torque can twist you off your feet!

Again, until you've got the heel/toe move mastered, let the upper torso follow the lower torso torque created by the turning of the feet...

As you gain spin proficiency, you can use your arm-spread to determine the speed of the spin (below, right).

Heel-Heel "Mohawk" Spin

This is a great way to **carve** a **turn** and/or bleed-off velocity.* If you lose it and fall you'll do a standard "**frontal fall**" inside your turn.

① Scissor inside skate to rear, preturn upper body & visualize the spin path. ② Unweight inside skate, turn it 180° and...

③ Reweight

Potential Spin Path

?

When your spin is complete, weight the leading skate, turn the trailing skate 180°, reweight both skates and you're done.

⑥

⑦

④ Using both inside edges, spin off vector.

⑤ The degree of inside lean determines speed loss due to friction: more lean, more friction → lower speed.

* See "Heel-Heel Braking Spin" pg. 113

124

"Back 2 Front"

So far you've seen about a dozen ways to go from skating forward to skating backward... Q: How do you turn back around without too much bloodshed? A: The "Back 2 Front" (or, for vocabularians, the "Back To Front.")

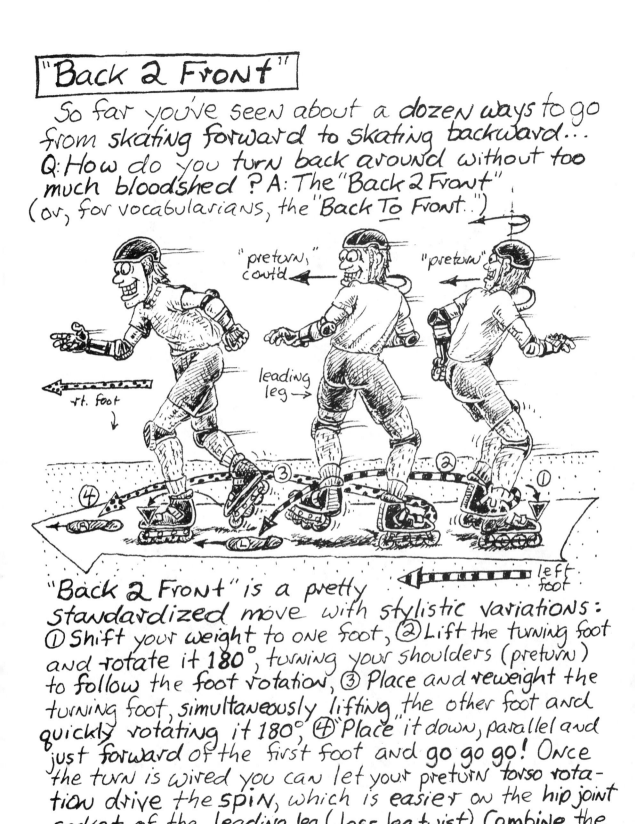

"Back 2 Front" is a pretty standardized move with stylistic variations: ① Shift your weight to one foot, ② Lift the turning foot and rotate it 180°, turning your shoulders (preturn) to follow the foot rotation, ③ Place and reweight the turning foot, simultaneously lifting the other foot and quickly rotating it 180°, ④ "Place" it down, parallel and just forward of the first foot and go go go! Once the turn is wired you can let your preturn torso rotation drive the spin, which is easier on the hip joint socket of the leading leg (less leg twist). Combine the "Back 2 Front" with a "Front 2 Back" for a cool 360° spin/turn (next two pages)!

* "place" - putting down precisely

Heel-Toe 360°
Spin

Front 2 Back
180°

Time

① ② ③ Side

Time

Front

126

Toe-Toe Pivot Spin

This is a very easy spin/turn technique. You simply rock onto your toe-wheels and pivot 180° "Front to Back". Preturning your upper body is recommended but optional. Scissoring is mandatory! (see below)

① Visualize spin path

Preturn upper torso *

Scissor

② ...up on toes...

Caution: if you fail to scissor before the pivot, your legs will become entangled and you will take a very colorful fall!

ha ha!

Yii!

What happens if you don't scissor...

③ ...pivot 180°

④ Follow thru by turning your head into the turn 'til you can see where you're going... (see "Linda Blair" move, pg. 29)

*Advanced skaters can "drive" the pivot with the preturn torque!

128

Heel-Heel Pivot Spin/Turn

This is a SLOW speed 180° spin, pivoting on the heel wheels while keeping your center of gravity over your toes. This is done by bringing your upper torso...

① preturn

C.O.G.

Scissor

② Pivot on heel-wheels 180°

center of gravity

②-A

yeek!

...forward over the toe wheels. If your center of gravity gets over the heel wheels, you execute a swift buttfall!

③ For maximum stability lift toes only ½" & smear your skates around 180°

C.O.G.

④

Since the heel pivot is destabilizing as a spin, you'll probably find it most useful as a low-speed vector turn for quick changes of direction.

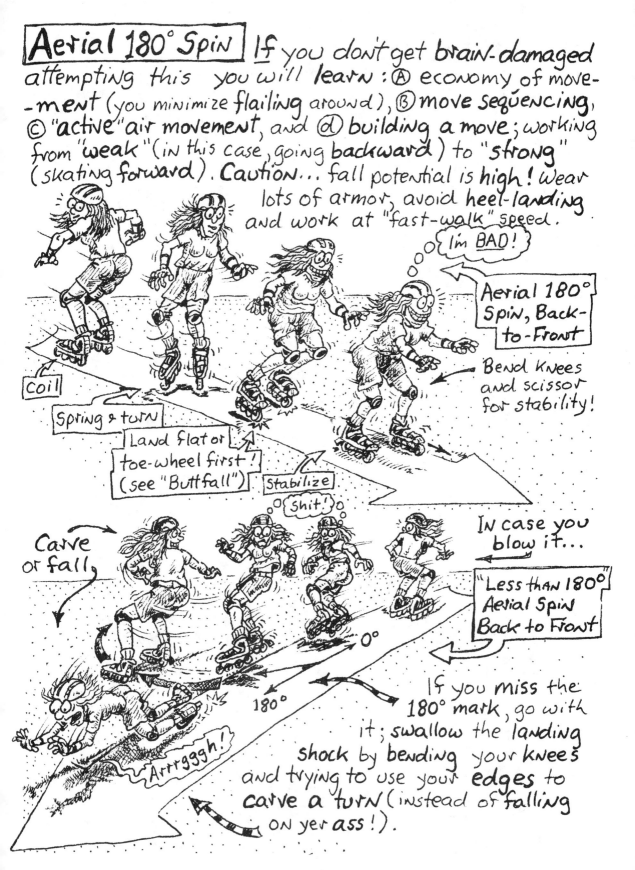

Aerial 180° Spin If you don't get brain-damaged attempting this you will learn: Ⓐ economy of move-ment (you minimize flailing around), Ⓑ move sequencing, Ⓒ "active" air movement, and ⓓ building a move; working from "weak" (in this case, going backward) to "strong" (skating forward). Caution... fall potential is high! Wear lots of armor, avoid heel-landing and work at "fast-walk" speed.

I'm BAD!

Aerial 180° Spin, Back-to-Front

Bend knees and scissor for stability!

Coil

Spring & turn

Land flat or toe-wheel first! (see "Buttfall")

Stabilize

Shit!

In case you blow it...

"Less than 180° Aerial Spin Back to Front

Carve or fall

0°

180°

Arrrgggh!

If you miss the 180° mark, go with it; swallow the landing shock by bending your knees and trying to use your edges to carve a turn (instead of falling on yer ass!).

Crossover Turns Crossover turning is a method for making a turn with minimal wheel-edge friction, which makes for a real fast turn! You minimize wheel friction by using the stepover (b&w arrow, below) to make the curve of your "turning circle" into a straight line. By stepping over, your skate takes the shortest path across the turn ("chord") and runs straight on the center "edge".. (wheel-edge friction zip!) to the next "corner" of the turn's curve. A 90° turn makes one corner, a 180° turn makes two or more corners. A 360° would look like a hexagon* from above (see below). Power comes from the "understroke"- the "inside" foot pushes to the outside of the turn, moving **under the body.**

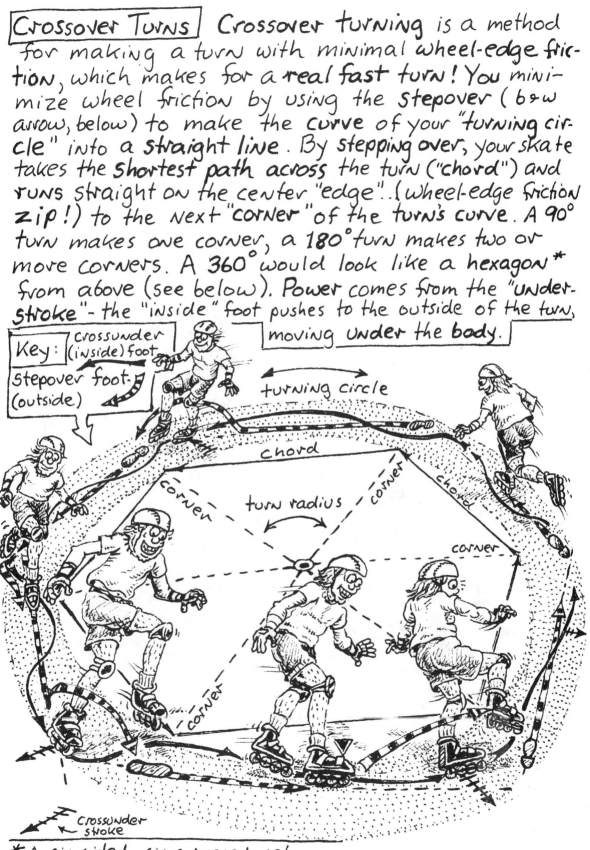

Key: crossunder (inside) foot
stepover foot (outside)

turning circle

chord

corner

turn radius

corner

chord

corner

corner

corner

crossunder stroke

*A six-sided, six cornered polygon

Crossover How To...

① Visualize the **arc** of the **turn**, begin "preturn...

② **Scissor** the **inside** foot forward (rt. foot, diagram),

③ Using the inside foot, begin a stroke to the **outside** of the turn while shifting **all** of your body weight onto that foot as it passes laterally **under** your body. This is the **first half** of the **crossunder stroke.** You'll want to end up **leaning** to the inside of the **turn**, balanced on the inside skate (which is now, technically the "outside" skate) so you

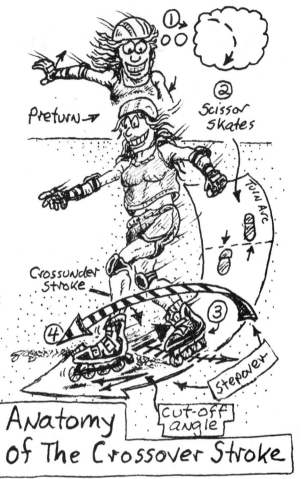

Anatomy of The Crossover Stroke

can **stepover** with the **actual** outside foot (left foot, diagram) ...**got that?** ④ **Stepover** - **lift** your recently **unweighted** outside foot **up** and **across** the **crossunder foot**, placing it **inside** the turn pointed so as to **cut across** the **arc** of your **turn** (step ② next page). Now you want to **shift** your weight **onto** the **stepover skate** as you **finish** your **crossunder** with a powerful, **body-weighted** **crossunder powerstroke** (step ③, next page). Now return your trailing "**crossunder skate**" back to **parallel**. **Repeat** as **necessary.** You should be going approximately the **same speed** **out** of the turn as you were **coming** **in**! Concentrate on keeping the stepover skate **upright** and on the **wheels' center "edges"** to avoid **losing** speed from **wheel edge friction** as you're **turning.** The **whole** move takes **only** 1 or 2 seconds!! Obviously it's **far easier** than you might think after reading the above text!

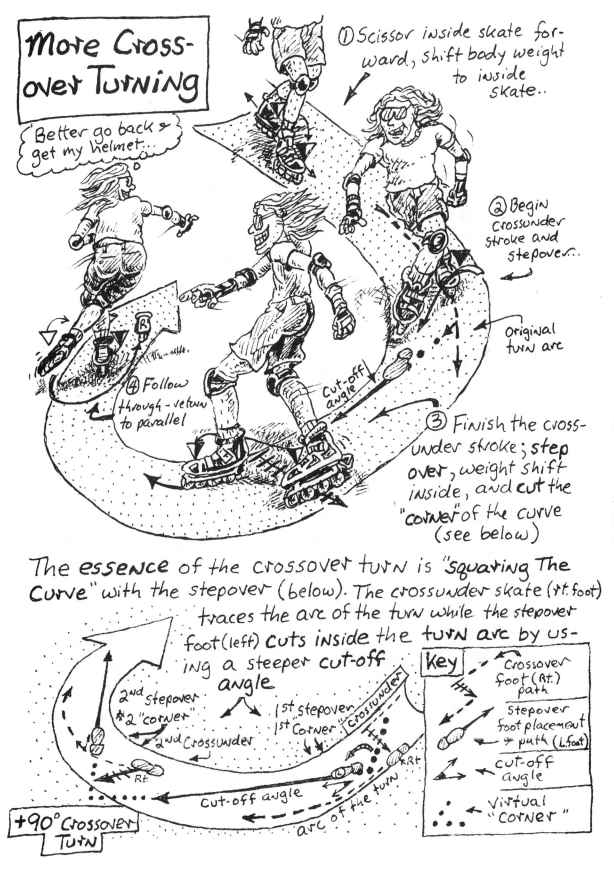

More Crossover Turning

"Better go back & get my helmet..."

① Scissor inside skate forward, shift body weight to inside skate..

② Begin crossunder stroke and stepover...

Original turn arc

③ Finish the crossunder stroke; step over, weight shift inside, and cut the "corner" of the curve (see below)

Cut-off angle

④ Follow through - return to parallel

The **essence** of the crossover turn is "squaring the Curve" with the stepover (below). The crossunder skate (rt. foot) traces the arc of the turn while the stepover foot (left) cuts inside the turn arc by using a steeper cut-off angle

2nd stepover #2 "corner"

2nd crossunder

1st stepover 1st "corner"

crossunder

cut-off angle

arc of the turn

Rt.

+90° Crossover Turn

Key
- Crossover foot (Rt.) path
- Stepover foot placement & path (L.foot)
- cut-off angle
- Virtual "corner"

133

Stepover Depth...

To tighten a turn, increase your stepover "depth" (@ & ®, below). By stepping deeper into a turn, you increase the cut-off angle across the curve. If you set your stepover skate too wide (©) you begin to <u>lose</u> speed from increased wheel-edge friction on the tilted crossunder skate. If you <u>want</u> to lose some speed intentionally (speed bleed), widen the stepover and relax your crossunder ankle to tilt your wheel edges to 30°-45°. You will slow down quickly! [this is a "crossunder brace/brake", covered in major detail at the end of this chapter...]

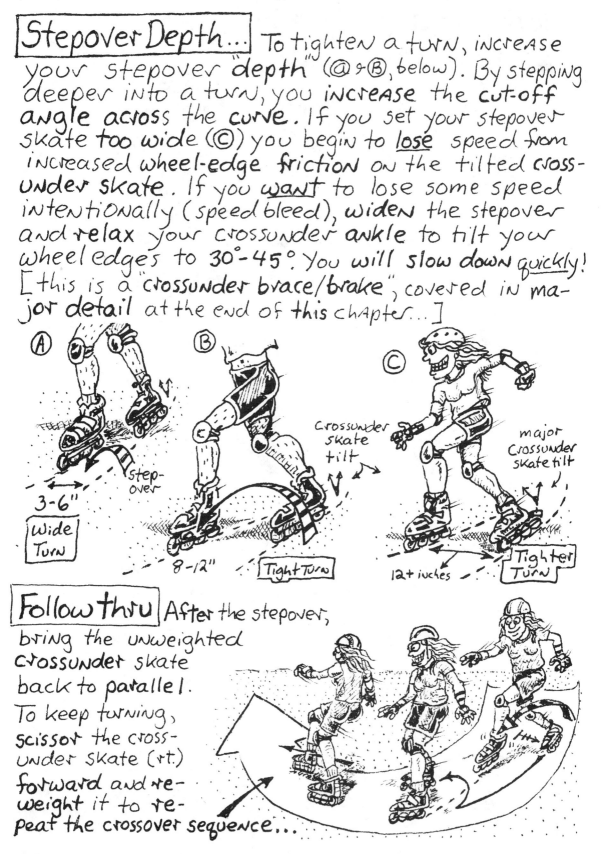

Ⓐ

step-over

3-6"

Wide Turn

Ⓑ

8-12"

Tight Turn

crossunder skate tilt

©

major crossunder skate tilt

12+ inches

Tighter Turn

Follow thru

After the stepover, bring the unweighted crossunder skate back to parallel.
To keep turning, scissor the cross-under skate (rt.) forward and re-weight it to repeat the crossover sequence...

A final **caution** on the "stepover"- If your stepover is **too deep**, your trailing skate will **roll out** and **shoot sideways**...

Detail

oo O !?

Yiiieeeeee!

A Break-free Point

stepover too wide!

...basically **flinging** you laterally off the turn vector via **centrifugal force!** Very dynamic...

Crossunder Caution | If you do like I did and try to do stepovers without **first** developing a **solid crossunder stroke**, you'll probably experience **numerous tangled leg wipe-outs** and the occasional **twisted ankle/knee** by lifting your crossunder skate's **heel** as you step-over which can torque the "**underfoot**" to the outside of the turn (see below). Read the crossunder portion of this chapter (next few pages) <u>before</u> attempting a crossover turn!

Underfoot Sprain

(yow!)

① Step-over

② Plant front foot which lifts crossunder skate's heel...

③ Twisting Fall

twisted ankle & knee

foot torque outside →

Tangled Leg Fall

135

Crossover/Crossunder Turn Comparison

① Scissor inside foot to **rear** & begin torso rotation into turn..

② Bring inside foot **under** body & push to **outside** of turn.

③ Shift weight to underfoot and push hard to **outside** of turn (understroke)..

④ Shift weight to leading foot and swizzle under-foot back inside to parallel form (retain slight scissor for extra stability).. Reweight inside foot

Understroke

Turn Apex

Yahoo!

Tighten

⑤ Optional- you can add an extra understroke to tighten your turn!

Crossunder Turn

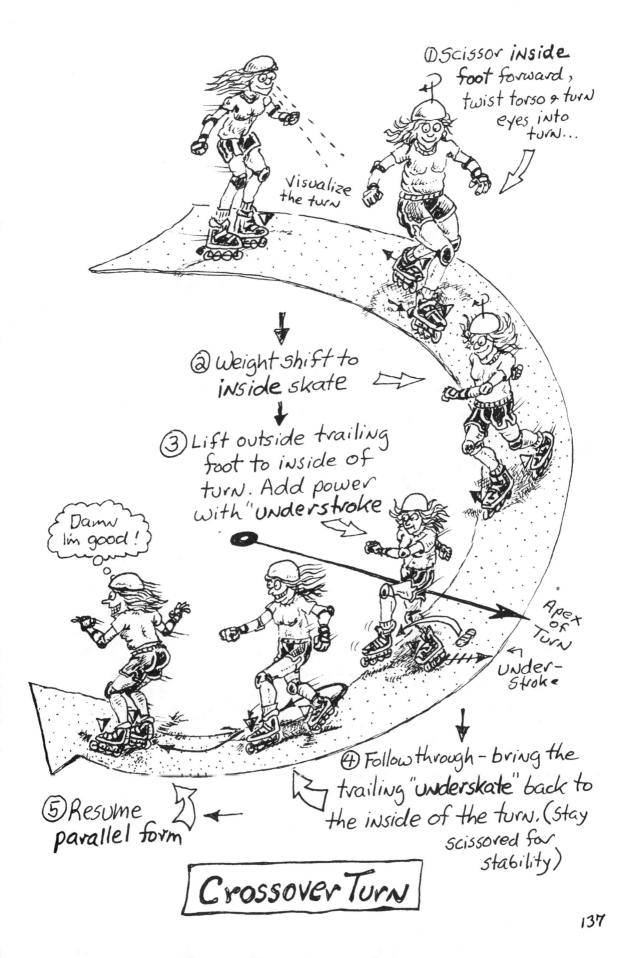

Crossover Turn

Crossunder Technique and Anatomy...

Whenever you're cross-scissoring your legs and using **one** skate as **both** an "inside" and "outside" skate, you're using **crossunder technique**. You can use it to **turn, glide,** and **brake** so it's **worth knowin'**. It's also the basis for **Switch-stance** and **mono-ski** styles (see "Style, pg.147).

weighted opposing foot

Cross Scissor

Outside Turn

Inside Turn

Understroke "IN"

Underskate or underfoot, (trailing foot)

Understroke (out)

Stance width

leading foot

Skate Angle

Crossunder Anatomy and Terminology

Crossunder Turn

① Scissor inside foot to rear.

② Weight under-foot

feet well-scissored!

Scissor inside foot rearward

Similar to first part of the cross-over turn except you **scissor** the **inside skate** to the **rear** first, eliminating the need for a **stepover** later. Shift weight to the rear "**underleg**" so you're balanced on an opposing leg and beginning a turn. (see ②)

In order for you to balance on an opposing foot, your under-skate will naturally **tilt** inside the turn, thus causing the turn. Use your leading skate (inside turn) to **steer** thru the turn or to simply **stabilize** your body over the **underskate** (opposite).

Underskate Tilt

Crossunder Technique

The Crossunder Turn radius is determined by the: ① "Angle-in" of your **leading skate**, ② width of your "under" stance, ③ **lean**, and ④ **Amount of drag** created by angling **toes out** on both skates causing sort of a **reverse snowplow** effect [optional]

Ⓐ Narrow stance
Ⓑ Skates running parallel...
Ⓒ Angle-in"

Wide Radius Turn

Ⓐ Leading foot angling in (heel "smear", Ⓑ Wide crossunder stance, Ⓒ Toes "out", and Ⓓ serious lean into turn...

Ⓓ Lean Angle
Ⓒ Toes Angled out
Radius
tilt
Ⓐ-Ⓑ - cutoff angle

Narrow Radius Turn

Your **overall speed** is determined by the strength of the understroke and whether or not your skates are parallel or angled out.

"Crisp" Short & powerful understroke

Narrow stance
Skates parallel or close to it

FAST

Ankle tilting further IN
Skates angled out
NO understroke

Wide Stance

"Crossunder Brake method" (Next pg.)

Slow(er)

*determines "cut-off angle".

139

Crossunder Powerbrake

Instead of "angling out" the underskate, relax ("break") your underfoot ankle and tilt your skate further onto its side to create major wheel-edge friction and bleed speed. By simultaneously widening your scissor stance and understroking hard to the outside, you can do a pretty good crossunder "powerslide". Be careful not to relax your ankle so much that the inside edge of your boot hits the ground; this will pry your wheels off the ground and you'll do a crossunder power-splat.

For more braking power, shift more and more weight from your inside skate to the sliding underskate. As awkward as this stance appears, it's fairly solid and the underfoot powerslide is quite effective!

puta!

! ¿! !

Ⓐ wt. shift "outside"
Ⓑ wide crossunder stance
Ⓒ understroke
Ⓓ Ankle "break"

How to Apply Crossunder Technique to the Crossover Turn Lesson...

Once you're feeling fairly solid doing wide, easy crossunder turns, practice picking up the unweighted outside skate as you do the understroke. Keep the "underknee" well bent! Once you can comfortably pick up the outside skate while understroking you're ready to do a decent stepover. By learning the crossunder first, you'll be relaxed and able to concentrate on stepover foot placement to cut-off the turn [and probably avoid a tangled legs fall!]

Lean

This might seem like a strange way to approach the crossover turn but this way you won't have to **unlearn** bad stepover technique if you learned the standard crossover **first**. Concentrate on precise stepover foot placement and a smooth reweighting of the foot after the stepover...

cut-off angle

⑤ reweight

① Scissor your "inside" foot forward...
② Weight shift to the underskate...
③ Understroke and lift your outside skate...
④ Stepover: good foot placement on the cut-off angle, & reweight.

① Scissor

②

③

④

Add move and more weight to your underfoot. Notice how merely weighting the underfoot initiates a turning motion...

Please turn back to the first few pages of this chapter for an exhaustive explication of "Stepovers"

③ (above)
④
⑤

Same Turn; front view Steps 3-5

From a solid, relaxed cross-under stance, bring the stepover foot inside the turn & reweight

Unweight

Understroke & Stepover

reweight

Crossunder "Switch-stance Style"

If you want a good overall velocity control system for cruising (especially downhill), linked alternating-sides crossunder speed bleeds are hard to beat. Slow down by widening your stance, speed up by bringing your skates closer together (below, L.).
To come to a complete stop, tilt your underskate "inside" and do a crossunder power slide (far right). This is a high-control downhill style!

scissor

bailout

powerslide

Once you've fried your legs doing linked turns, you can micro-rest by tucking the under-knee in behind the leading knee and relaxing the underleg, resting in the knee pocket (of the front leg).

Ahhh... ooo

Faster

Slower

STANCE WIDTH

142

At medium to high **speeds**, when <u>not falling</u> becomes highly important, Nestle your underleg knee in the pocket behind the leading knee. This forces you to keep your knees **well-bent.** It also provides a great NON-VISUAL anchor point when you're having to focus your attention elsewhere!

Yo!

!

The **knee tuck** also **stabilizes** the lower legs, eliminating **skate wobble** and "**Elvis Legs**" at high velocities.

When your legs are blown there is a tendency to **straighten** the under leg & **rest on bone*** instead of leg muscles; this also puts your weight toward the **heel** of the **under foot**, setting you up for a very colorful loss of control.

Ahhh

yiiieee!

Elvis Legs...

Leg Locked

Foom!

THUD.

① ② ③

*skeletal support

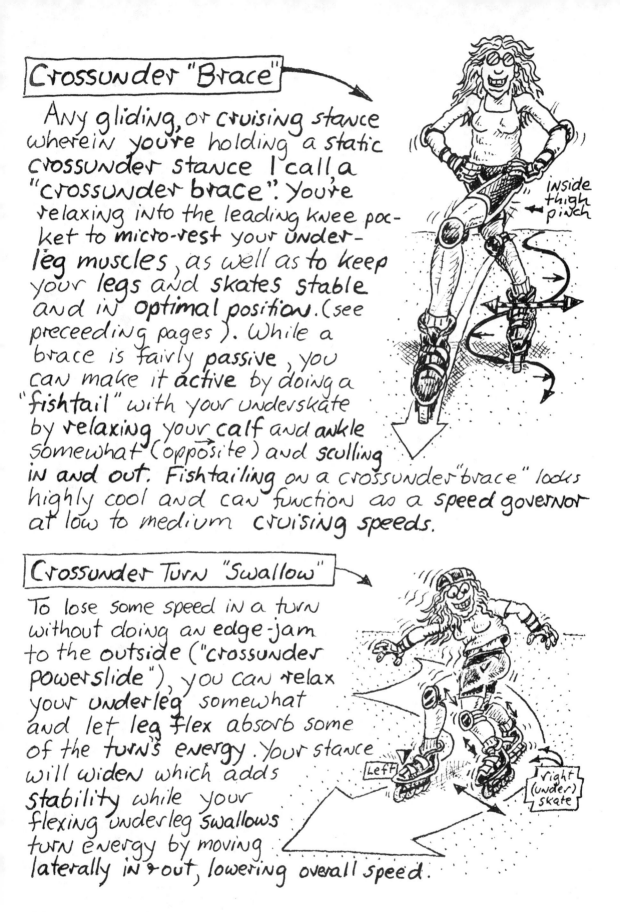

Crossunder "Brace"

Any gliding, or cruising stance wherein you're holding a static crossunder stance I call a "crossunder brace". You're relaxing into the leading knee pocket to micro-rest your under-leg muscles, as well as to keep your legs and skates stable and in optimal position. (see preceeding pages). While a brace is fairly passive, you can make it active by doing a "fishtail" with your underskate by relaxing your calf and ankle somewhat (opposite) and sculling in and out. Fishtailing on a crossunder "brace" looks highly cool and can function as a speed governor at low to medium cruising speeds.

inside thigh pinch

Crossunder Turn "Swallow"

To lose some speed in a turn without doing an edge-jam to the outside ("crossunder powerslide"), you can relax your underleg somewhat and let leg flex absorb some of the turn's energy. Your stance will widen which adds stability while your flexing underleg swallows turn energy by moving laterally in & out, lowering overall speed.

Left

right (under) skate

Advanced "Cut Turn"

Pivot *

Turn

Vector

① ②

Rear View

Backwards Crossunder-

This is an advanced-intermediate skill! Begin by doing hard-edged cutturns on one side (above). After each cut, bring the now-trailing skate back to parallel in a sculling motion. From above, the backwards crossunder footwork looks like linked offset backwards swizzle strokes* Make sure you scissor longways so you don't tangle your legs on the crossunder stroke. Wear Armor- you will fall..... sculling ...learning this stroke! Once you've got the basic footwork wired, concentrate on both feet smoothly sculling in & out from a "fixed scissor" body position/stance.

L Rt.

cut turn

L cut turn 2

Rt.

sculling

② ①

R L R L

R L

R L

* Just like swizzling, your wheels remain grounded throughout!

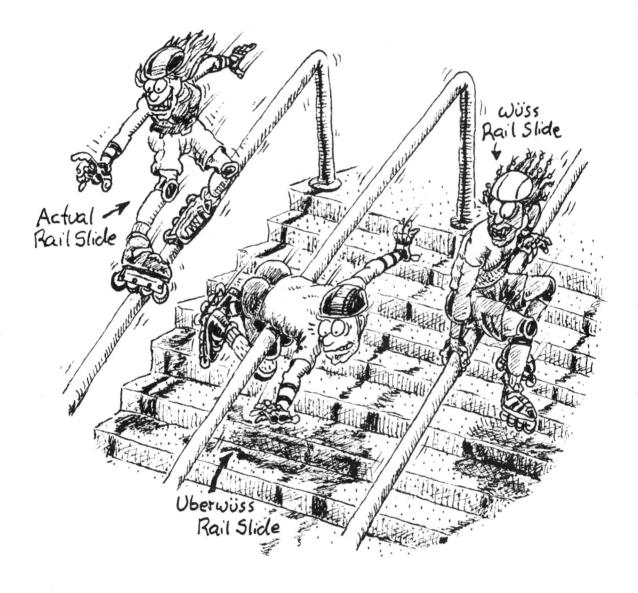

Actual
Rail Slide

Wüss
Rail Slide

Uberwüss
Rail Slide

Style

Style is not just looks! It's the artful combination of individual moves & skills into unified, flowing movement. When developing unified movement, the skater learns to drive his/her skates **aggressively** * (active/directive style vs. passive "style"). Ultimately, this directed flow plus skill becomes instinctive (body memory) ...then you've got some **real style**! Using this **aggressive/directed flow** will make you a safer skater; you're acting in anticipation (not reaction) and **you, not** the terrain, are calling the shots. Style focuses on **process**, not freeze-frame, two-dimensional **poses**. You want to begin thinking in **arcs** and **circles** (not straight lines) and **four dimensions**! (next page)

Oi! ?oo

Fall Line

Tons 'o Style

No Style Whatsoever

* "Drive your skates or they drive you!"

The Age Of Tubism*
(Skating & Thinking In Four Dimensions...

Since we skate in a four dimensional world (length, width, height, plus time [below, right]) it's beneficial to learn to see and think four dimensionally to ana-**lyze** and appreciate skating moves in order to learn how to do 'em. If you think

"Dude Descending A Staircase"

about a move sequence only in terms of the "peak move" (below) you may get slapped by the planet because you forgot you had to land! If you "see" move sequences as a "tube of movement" you're going to fit your airborne body **through***, you'll have anticipated landing as well as take-off and flight. This is the cinematic version of "move sequencing"!

Peak move
ga!

3 Dimensions ⤴
4 Dimensions ⤵

"peak move"

* 4th Dimensional Movement "Tube"

Time

height

width

Length

*Apologies to Marcel Duchamp
148

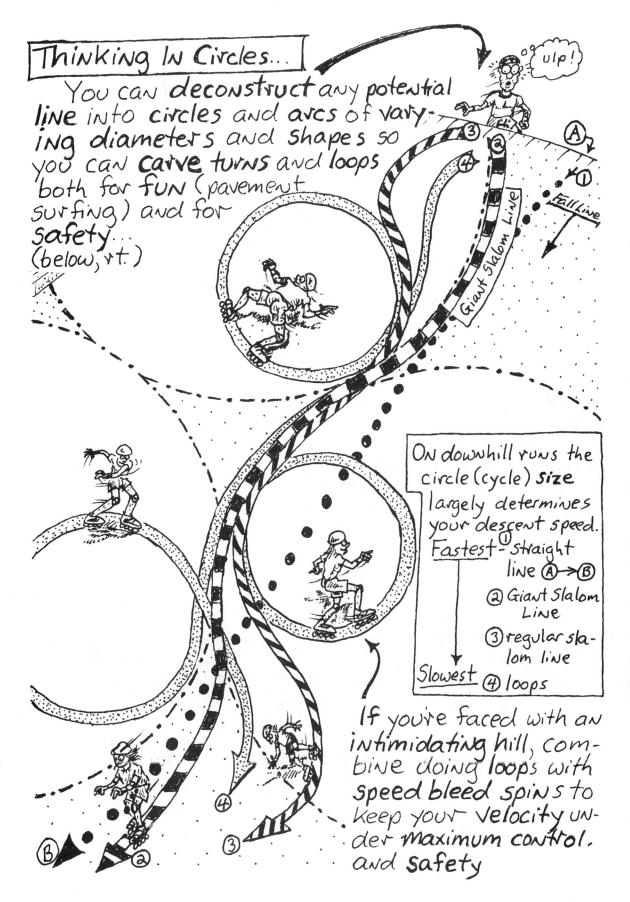

Thinking In Circles...

You can **deconstruct** any potential **line** into **circles** and **arcs** of varying **diameters** and **shapes** so you can **carve turns** and **loops** both for **fun** (pavement surfing) and for **safety**... (below, rt.)

On downhill runs the circle (cycle) **size** largely determines your descent speed. <u>Fastest</u>- straight line Ⓐ→Ⓑ
② Giant Slalom Line
③ regular slalom line
<u>Slowest</u> ④ loops

If you're faced with an **intimidating** hill, combine doing **loops** with **speed bleed spins** to keep your **velocity** under **maximum control**. and **safety**

"MONO-SKI" or "Surfin'" style

This is probably the most amusing style for good old-fashioned "Sidewalk Surfing!"

This style consists of running your skates in line, literally. Turns & spins are done with body torque & leans; your feet remain semi-fixed in line except to scissor one in front of the other (stance switch).

Kowabunga!

Scissor

"Inside Turn"

"Outside" Turn

Excellent for pedestrian slalom!

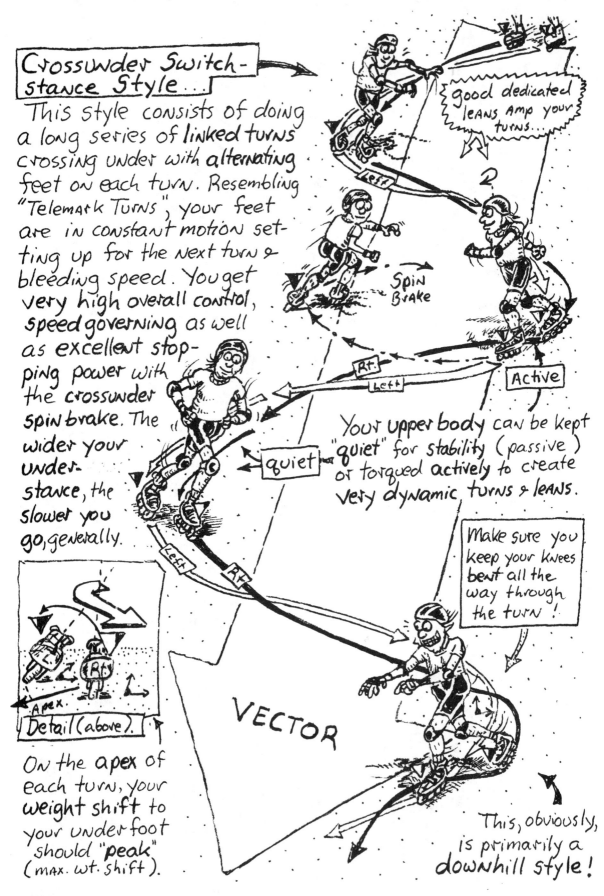

Crossunder Switch-stance Style...

This style consists of doing a long series of *linked turns* crossing under with **alternating feet** on each turn. Resembling "Telemark Turns", your feet are in constant motion setting up for the next turn & bleeding speed. You get very high overall control, **speed governing** as well as excellent stopping power with the **crossunder spin brake**. The wider your understance, the slower you go, generally.

On the **apex** of each turn, your **weight shift** to your underfoot should "**peak**" (max. wt. shift).

good dedicated leans Amp your turns...

Spin Brake

Active

Rt. / Left

Your upper body can be kept "quiet" for stability (passive) or torqued actively to create very dynamic turns & leans.

quiet

Left / Rt.

Apex

Detail (above).

VECTOR

Make sure you keep your knees bent all the way through the turn!

This, obviously, is primarily a **downhill style!**

Crossunder Switch-stance Style...

When necessary you can add some *parallel* style to create *new vectors*.

Parallel

New Vector

Good speed control & way-flashy!

Because this style is relatively narrow and gives you excellent control, it's ideal for negotiating downgrades cluttered with "soft" organic obstacles.

Detail: crossunder weight distribution* on apex of turn...

80%

20%

L   R

*percentages Approximate, fool!

For more information on Switchstance Style, see pg.142

153

More Crossunder Switch-stance Style...

If you're over-angling* the underskate on the apex of the turn, said skate can **break loose** causing a twisting fall. At the very least, your **boot** gets **abraided**...

Yiiieee!

Skeee-rrrunch!

Ahhh..

unweight & relax "off leg"

micro-rest

This is also a good **micro-rest** method at **low speeds**, level or downhill. You transfer most of your weight onto your **underfoot** and unweight your **leading** foot for a few **restful** seconds...

damn!

Eeeek!

R L

SCREECH!

Using the crossunder switch **stance**, you are almost constantly in braking po- **sition**, making quick stops — or evasive maneuvers relatively easy. Done right you can execute an actual **crossunder hockey-stop**. Done wrong and you woof it! As usual, practice makes perfect.

*Or running too-hard durometer wheels for move.

154

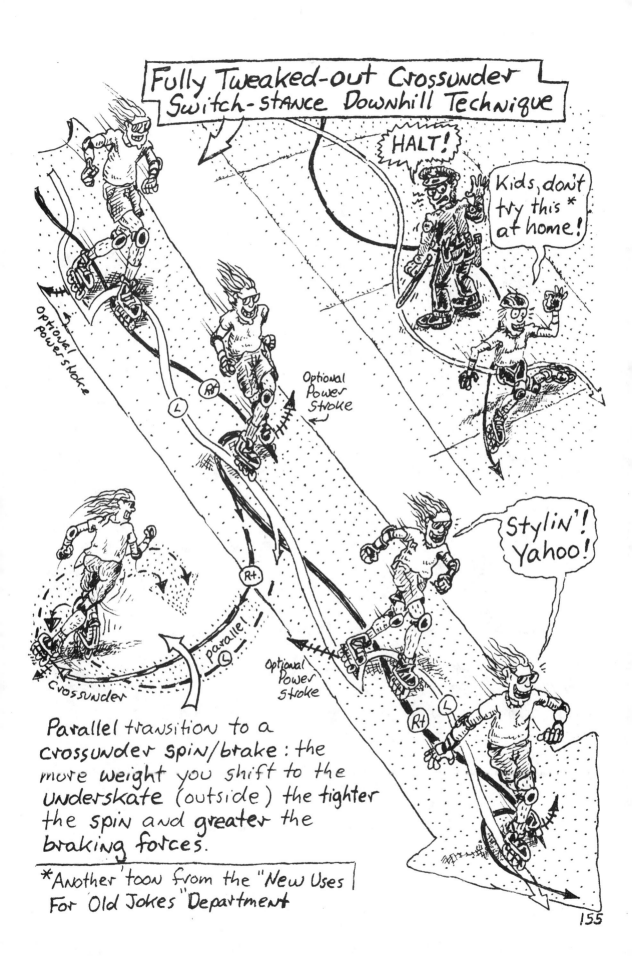

Parallel transition to a crossunder spin/brake: the more weight you shift to the underskate (outside) the tighter the spin and greater the braking forces.

*Another 'toon from the "New Uses For Old Jokes" Department

Style Survival Tips

TRANSITION

Level Transition

Head level

Shit!

Knees not bent!

Knees Bent, stable

Unbent knees: UNSTABLE!

Knees Bent, stable

level transition, very stable

"Transition Instability" - Whenever you're switching stances, doing linked crossunders, etc. AVOID rising up and un-bending your knees! Anytime your legs are straightened out, resting "skeletally", you have absolutely NO shock absorption, high center of gravity, etc. Bent knee transitions can be tricky but you'll avoid considerable road rash by keeping those knees bent!

Head Level

Watch those surface con-ditions when doing big leans, turn carving, etc.! If you hit gravel, or car snot* or if you're running too-hard' wheels, you'll go flying off the planet, which is Never very stylish.

merde!

─────────────────

*crankcase drippings   'durometer

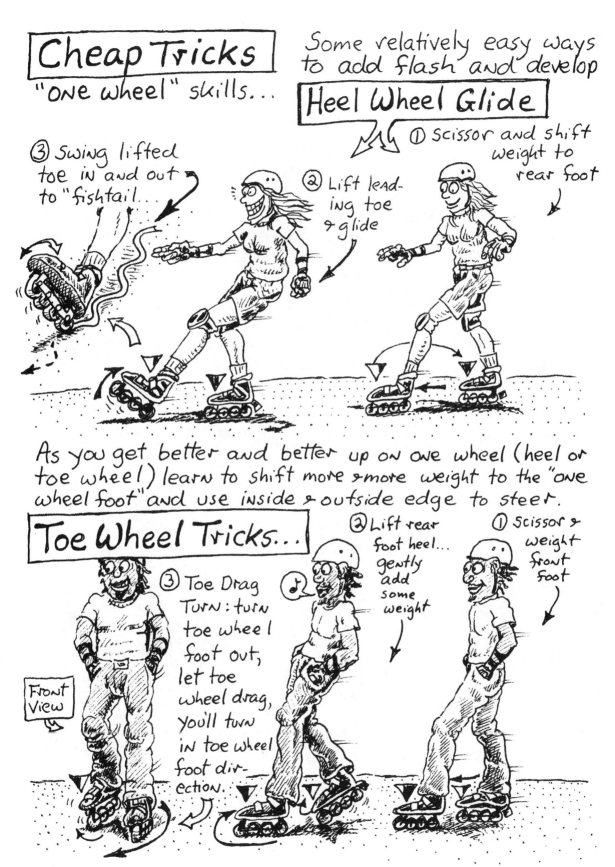

Cheap Tricks
"one wheel" skills...

Some relatively easy ways to add flash and develop

Heel Wheel Glide

① scissor and shift weight to rear foot

③ Swing lifted toe in and out to "fishtail...

② Lift leading toe & glide

As you get better and better up on one wheel (heel or toe wheel) learn to shift more & more weight to the "one wheel foot" and use inside & outside edge to steer.

Toe Wheel Tricks...

② Lift rear foot heel... gently add some weight

① scissor & weight front foot

③ Toe Drag Turn: turn toe wheel foot out, let toe wheel drag, you'll turn in toe wheel foot direction.

Front View

By wiggling the toe wheel skate in and out you can **fishtail flashily** and, by further weighting the toe wheel skate, actually **steer** in wide slalom arcs ⟹

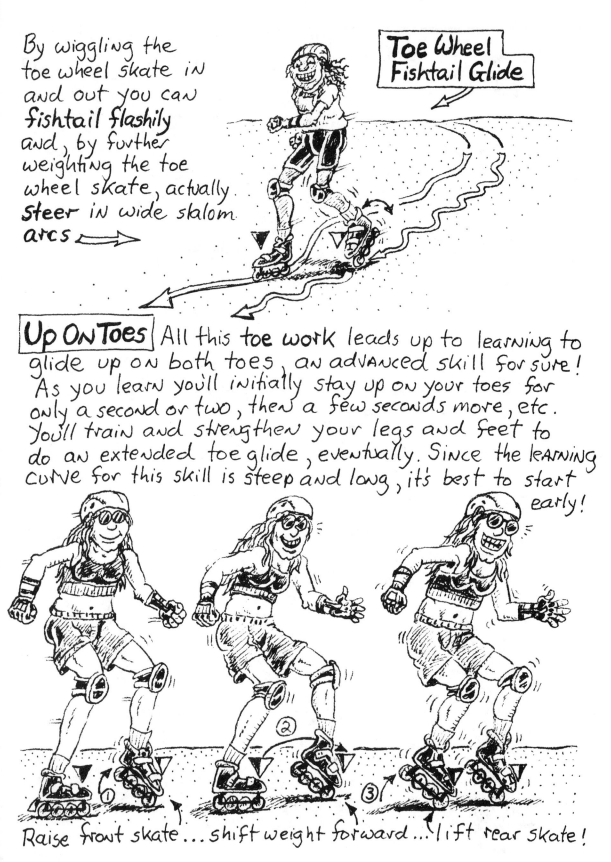

Toe Wheel Fishtail Glide

Up On Toes All this **toe work** leads up to learning to glide up on both toes, an advanced skill for sure! As you learn you'll initially stay up on your toes for only a second or two, then a few seconds more, etc. You'll train and strengthen your legs and feet to do an extended toe glide, eventually. Since the learning curve for this skill is steep and long, it's best to start early!

Raise front skate... shift weight forward... lift rear skate!

Stealth Skating

Here's a style that's actually functional! You want to appear to NON-skaters to be walking, not rolling...it's kinda like a reverse "moonwalk" A very handy style to have when exploring new territory; you can blend in with the other bipeds... under the radar!

☆SHOES☆

SALE!

Victorias Secret

slide

micro-push

Tuck your helmet under your arm!

Props like shopping bags & baggy pants work great!

It's kinda like a gliding shuffle... go real slow!

③

②

①

toe-wheel "front" step

micro-push

Stealth "Walking"

159

Basic Mechanics...

Welcome To Skate City

Basic mechanics...

Learning to be your own mechanic saves time and $$! It's so **easy** a **klutz** like me can master it...

"lower" — strap — CUFF — "upper" — brake — brake pad — "active" brake mechanism

frame — wheels

wheel — cased bearings — hub — bearing spacer — "bearing assembly" — Axle — Axle nut

5/32 allen (4mm works in a pinch)

The bearing assembly can be further subdivided into...

casing

retaining spring — cap — cap — ret. spring — bearings * — frame

"Unsealed bearings"

To service wheels and bearings you will need: two 5/32 allen wrenches, cleaning (degreasing) solution, oil and an assortment of rags, Q-tips and such. A notebook is useful for diagramming disassembly steps so you'll be able to put it all back together correctly. Skates also have brake sub-assemblies, rocker spacers, etc. that go flying everywhere when the wheels come off (see below). A fairly clean work area is good for recovering flying parts more easily. In short, **don't** take your wheels apart in the **grass**! A few clean utility bowls can come in pretty handy for keeping parts together at various stages of the procedure...

F-word!

PING!

*Do not attempt to remove bearings from casing!! Trust me on this...

Half the job of overhauling wheels is patience and good organization. First, loosen the axle nuts, remove axles and stack your wheels nearby in order of reassembly [see "Wheel Rotation," pg. 166]. I've found that

a row of four stacks of two wheels works well (left). Label the wheel stack (rt. skate, left skate, toe direction, etc.) to avoid confusion later. Push (never pry) your bearing casings and spacers out of the wheel hubs, restacking wheels in order as you go. Drop all metal parts (bearings, axles, axle nuts, etc.) into a bowl of degreaser solution to soak. While the metal parts are soaking, take a degreaser-dampened rag and cotton swabs and clean the plastic parts as well as the bottoms of both the boots including the wheel frames and brake assembly.

Pick out a few random bearing assemblies and try "test spinning". If the bearing is frozen (won't spin) or only sort of spins while making a crunch-crunch crunch noise, you probably are in need of a total bearing casing subassembly overhaul, only if your bearings are of the servicable variety. You can try resoaking and hand-spinning each bearing to flush out the grit, crud, and muck binding the bearings...

sometimes this works, usually not!

[Bearing Casing Subassembly] Take a sharp pointy object (such as a small finishing nail, needle, jewelers screwdriver, etc.) and pop out the retaining spring on each side of the casing. Remove both endcaps and drop the whole mess back into the degreaser jar. Apply bandaids over all the holes you just punched in your left digits with the sharp...

pointy "retaining spring extraction device". After this first overhaul you won't stab yourself nearly so often, really! Think about all the wonderful satisfaction you're going to experience if you can somehow manage to get your *!*?(skates cleaned up and reassembled correctly without killing yourself or others...

Ee-Yow!

damn!

Once you've brushed, blown, spun, and swabbed all the gook out of your bearings, spin dry and allow all parts to dry thoroughly. Any drops of liquid degreaser you fail to blot up can break down the new lubrication, rendering all your efforts utterly useless. Similarly, if you used a brush to clean your bearings and bearing frames, check carefully to make sure you didn't leave brush bristles jammed between bearings and frames. Reassembly: Replace one end cap and retaining spring on each bearing casing. If you're a greaser,* pack with grease or, for best results, soak with bearing oil. Add the second end-cap and test spin each overhauled assembly to make double sure all the grit is gone [if you used nasty grease, the bearing probably will not spin at this stage]. If all the bearings spin silently and smoothly, add the bearing spacer and replace in the wheel hubs. Once completely reassembled, spin again: greased bearings should now spin easily (pushed by the mass of the wheel) and oiled bearings should roll and roll. Wipe all excess oil off the wheel's tread surface and remount wheels in the frames according to your preselected wheel rotation order (remember?). I like to tighten my wheels until they noticably slow down then back off (loosen) one "click." Be sure to tighten at least one more time before you skate on them...there's always some slack in any reassembled wheel configuration. If you're...

* Anti-grease bias warning! I believe grease gums up and holds grit in the bearings, mucking up your bearings over time!

lubricating with oil, always try to store & transport your skates upright so the oil doesn't leak out of your bearing races*. If you're not going to skate on your newly rebuilt wheels immediately, spin the wheels daily to ensure a good coat of oil on your bearings until you resume skating.

Finally, take a look around your work area... if you find any "spare parts" lying around, it's appropriate to scream and have a minor breakdown. Being as there are no "spare parts" on most inline skates, you now must find where the part belongs... sort of a mechanical skate dissection!

Aiiieeee!

★!?✻

However

If you're not too badly in-jured (by the retaining spring extraction device, of course!) and the reinstalled wheels actually roll smoothly, and there are no spare parts left over, congratulations! The next time will be easier. Have a couple beers, you deserve it!

yo! I did it!

whirrrrrrrrr...

Honkin' Big Sewing Needle

Homemade Retaining Spring Extraction Device
Find a humongous sewing needle and, using pliers, press the dull end into a pencil-size section of dowel. Practice "retaining spring extraction" by stabbing yourself in the left palm, thumb, & digits!

* The inside circumference of bearing casing.

165

Wheel Rotation Configurations

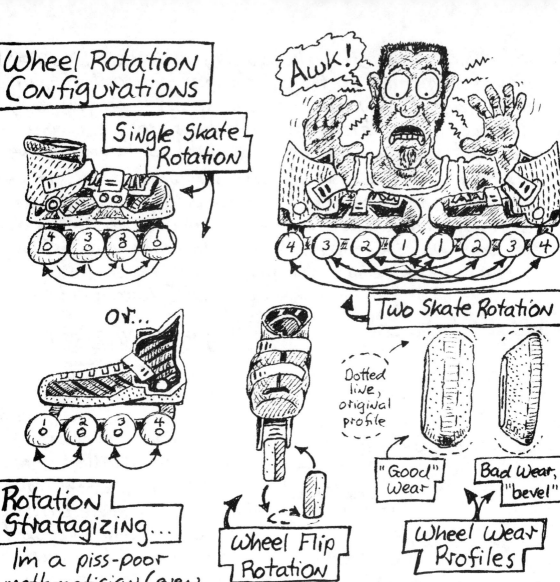

Single Skate Rotation

4 3 2 1

Awk!

Two Skate Rotation

4 3 2 1 1 2 3 4

or...

1 2 3 4

Wheel Flip Rotation

Dotted line, original profile

"Good" Wear

Bad Wear, "bevel"

Wheel Wear Profiles

Rotation Stratagizing...

I'm a piss-poor mathmatician (even by cartoonist standards!) but, according to my calculations, there are twenty-four possible wheel configurations on a single 4 wheel skate. Add in skate to skate cross rotation and wheel flips and things start gettin' real exponential. The simplest and most common rotation schedule is "toe wheel to heel, move #2, #3, & #4 forward one space" (above, upper left). The specific schedule you end up using is less important than actually performing frequent wheel rotations. In other words, tossing your wheels in a paper bag and remounting them at random is better than the most complex, scientific two-skate criss-cross wheel-flip system as long as you actually do the rotation act! If the system is too complicated,

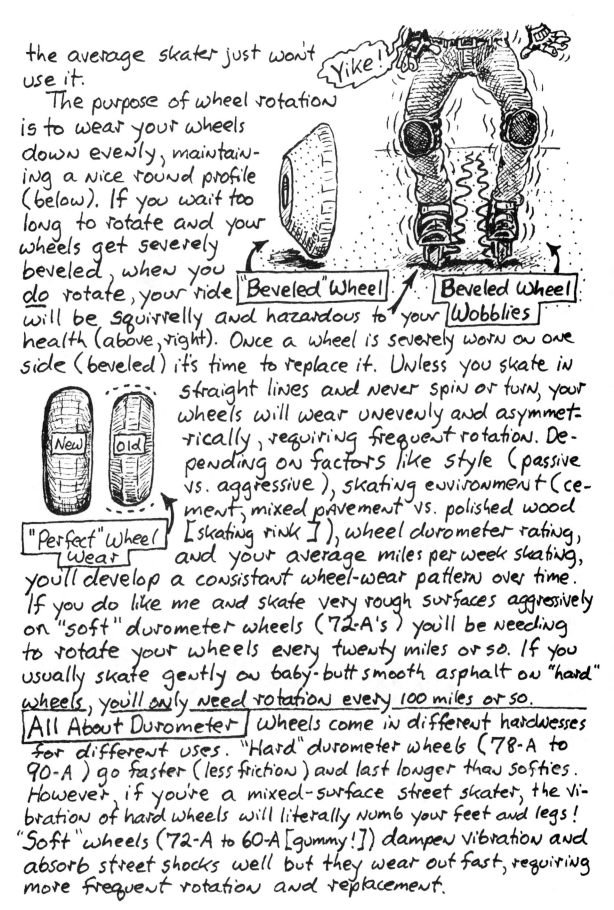

the average skater just won't use it.

The purpose of wheel rotation is to wear your wheels down evenly, maintaining a nice round profile (below). If you wait too long to rotate and your wheels get severely beveled, when you do rotate, your ride will be squirrelly and hazardous to your health (above, right). Once a wheel is severely worn on one side (beveled) it's time to replace it. Unless you skate in straight lines and never spin or turn, your wheels will wear unevenly and asymmetrically, requiring frequent rotation. Depending on factors like style (passive vs. aggressive), skating environment (cement, mixed pavement vs. polished wood [skating rink]), wheel durometer rating, and your average miles per week skating, you'll develop a consistant wheel-wear pattern over time. If you do like me and skate very rough surfaces aggressively on "soft" durometer wheels (72-A's) you'll be needing to rotate your wheels every twenty miles or so. If you usually skate gently on baby-butt smooth asphalt on "hard" wheels, you'll only need rotation every 100 miles or so.

"Yike!"

"Beveled" Wheel

Beveled Wheel

Wobblies

New   Old

"Perfect" Wheel Wear

All About Durometer   Wheels come in different hardnesses for different uses. "Hard" durometer wheels (78-A to 90-A) go faster (less friction) and last longer than softies. However, if you're a mixed-surface street skater, the vibration of hard wheels will literally numb your feet and legs! "Soft" wheels (72-A to 60-A [gummy!]) dampen vibration and absorb street shocks well but they wear out fast, requiring more frequent rotation and replacement.

167

soft". Hard Wheels: 80a "med. hard", 90a "very hard".
Recreational street skaters generally use hardnesses of
72a → 78a. Performance of "soft" vs. "hard" wheels are;
The "softer" the wheels, the ① slower, ② less-durable
(more wheel rotations required), ③ smoother the ride
(very important under "street" conditions!), ④ more maneuverable, ⑤ more traction[1] (but slippery when wet; they
can also soak up crankcase drippings, excess bearing
lube oil, etc. More porous).

1. Caution - radical smears
and/or vector-perpendic-
ular slide moves can
result in "velcroing" wherein
the sliding/smearing wheels
suddenly stick, sending
you flying ass-over-elbows...

Yaaah!

Velcroed!

Hard Wheels are... ① faster,
② more durable (less wheel rotations required), ③ rougher
riding (s'ess shock absorption), ④ less maneuverable (less
"grip"), ⑤ slippery on smooth surfaces (wheels can
break free on a turn and skid, which is great fun if
done intentionally) and extremely slippery
on wet or dewy pavement!!

③

Wheel Size - (diameter)
"big" wheels. 76mm+
are faster* than
little
bitty
wheels,
70mm or less.

⑤

Power Skiddin'!

*counterintuitive but true!

Bearings

Your bearings are arguably <u>the</u> most important component of the skate "system". The type "sealed" [not servicable] vs. "unsealed" [user servicable, see p.g. 162], grade (ABEC *, below), and the condition of your bearings more than anything else affects your skates' performance!

Bearings are graded by the "ABEC" standard which reflects the technical roundness of each ball bearing. For example, ABEC-5's are machined to tolerances of $\frac{1}{10,000}$ th of an inch or so. The rounder the ball bearing, the less friction in the system and the faster you can go. I recommend using unsealed ABEC-3's or higher. Unrated bearings make good fishing sinkers.

ABEC-1	"acceptable"	suitable for beginners
ABEC-3	"faster"	" " intermediates
ABEC-5	"very fast"	" " intermediates & up
ABEC-7	"ultra fast"	" " " racerheads
ABEC-9	"too fast:" experimental...must be made under		

zero-gravity conditions (space) for perfect center of gravity!

You can also upgrade your bearing spacers (plastic to metal), axle assemblies, etc. to similarly high technical specifications but it can get expensive and turn you into a techno-weenie real quick. My girlfriend says "Upgrading isn't technological evolution, it's a **disease**!" Besides, until you're fairly experienced as a skater, you won't be able to feel the difference between original equipment and an upgrade anyway...

Wheels

Skate wheels also come in a baffling array of styles, sizes, compositions, and profiles. For the average skater, two things really matter: **Wheel Size** * & Durometer - the hardness of the wheel's tread surface (rubber (soft) → turbo-plastic composite (hard). Durometer is expressed as a number followed by an "a".

<u>Soft wheels</u>: 68a, <u>70a (very soft)</u>, 72a-74a "medium

* Wheel Size discussed on next page.

169

Street Mechanics

Before you go skating, take a couple minutes to check out your skates mechanically. A lost wheel or messed up brake can have a very bad effect on your skating experience _and_ health! The two main things to check are: ① Wheels- make sure the axle bolts are tight so your wheels stay on! But not so tight they don't spin freely...

Preskate Tune Up

Tools & Parts: the bare minimum
Ⓐ 5/32 Allen wrench
Ⓑ Spare brake pad
Ⓒ Spare axle & cap
Ⓓ assorted spacers, Ⓔ Cut-down screwdriver for brake repair/adjust (phillips head or reg.)
Ⓕ waist pouch or fanny pack to put it all in.

② Brake-Make sure your brake pad has some rubber left on it. Carry a spare brake pad in case you fry the old one (a common problem in hilly territory!). If you've got active brakes make sure the lever is working and the device is properly adjusted. Most brakes usually require only a screwdriver (phillips or regular) to adjust and service. Check before skating to ensure you're carrying the correct tool.

Lost Axle/Wheel Protocol

This is the most common "ruin-your-day" mechanical problem! If you neglect occasional axle tightening your axle cap will loosen and fall off, followed moments later by the axle working its way out and your wheel coming off. You'll probably recover the axle but the axle nut is 50 yards to a mile behind you somewhere, as are your rocker spacers as well. If you brought your spare axle assembly and spacers, bolt the wheel back on and _NOW_ check the other wheels for tightness.

Axle Nut

Axle · spare spacers

The good news is, even if you forgot the spare axle, you only need four wheels (of eight!) to roll! Your skates may vibrate like hell and feel like tiny grocery carts but you can **keep skating** using creative auto-cannibalization. Just make sure you've got a toe and heel wheel on each skate and you're good to go!

Nnnnnno ppppppppproblem!

4 Wheelin'

{!} In the course of messing about with your wheels & brake, you've probably noticed that the axle on the heel of your brake skate is a bit longer than the others. If you lose this axle you're <u>screwed</u> so carry a spare if at all possible. You can, with incredible difficulty, actually skate with only the three forward wheels in place but walking is easier and far less humiliating...

Other Accessories...

For skate touring and other forms of skate adventurism, you may want to carry: ① sunglasses, ② a water bottle, ③ a daypack for all these accessories, ④ flip flops or sneakers for "no skating" areas (cafés, museums, subways, etc.). Most cabbies don't care if you're wearing skates as long as you are white.

⑤ Pepper spray (illegal in some areas!) effective against bad dogs, muggers, hare Krishnas and racist cabbies!

⑥ "throw-down wallet" - disposable wallet containing a few small bills but NO credit cards or I.D. If you get mugged, toss 'em the wallet and haul butt! Do like mama said and keep your money in your sock!... and ⑦ street map.

① Sunglasses
② water bottle
③ daypack
④ flip flops
⑤ pepper spray
⑥ "Throw-down" wallet
⑦ street map
$$

171

The Inevitable Benediction...

You may have noticed that in the popular media (television in particular) inline skating is used to depict outrageously risky behavior by medical liability lawyers, first care/rehab centers, insurance companies, and other commercial interests (the "adrenaline media", etc.).

In TV commercials skating is shown to be even more dangerous than driving drunk and chain-smoking while talking on a cell phone to a 900 number live phone sex operator!

Well, I doth protest... blading can't be all that dangerous

...'cause I'm a notoriously clumsy, unathletic blader with a lot less common sense than most would even consider to be "normal" and I'm not dead yet(!). A little "road rash" but no real "injuries"* Perhaps it's the helmet and body armor I wear, or luck... or both. I hate wearing a helmet + pads just as much as the next guy, but it is a proven fact that

it is very difficult to push the skating envelope from a hospital bed! Besides, as Wino Bob says "... there's a bunch o' better ways to destroy yer brain cells than hittin' yer head on the danged sidewalk...hic!"

Inline skating being the ultra-macho warrior culture that it is, fear isn't mentioned too often but here goes: "I'm a big dumb hairy guy and sometimes, under certain conditions (high speed + cruddy pavement + lots of cars), I get scared shitless!" Not nearly as often as when I was just starting + getting hammered a lot but fear still happens on occasion. My "advanced-intermediate fear" is of the "heightened awareness of one's immediate environment" variety and is almost a meditative trance state, not the "paralyzed-and-fixin'-to-puke" fear of my beginner days. Sometimes fear is just good judgement in an adrenaline package, worth paying attention to but never allowed to be a limit. Fear can be actually enjoyed as a heightened state of consciousness with enhanced physical capabilities brought on by a healthy blast of adrenaline and dopamine! That's right... FEAR CAN BE FUN!

* I haven't been so lucky in other "thrill" sports...

174

A final issue of great importance to all skaters is access to skating territory (i.e. - parks, malls, streets, sidewalks, etc.). Obnoxious skater behavior is generally rewarded with **loss of access** (!) so pl<u>ease</u> skate in control and be as nice as you can to non-skaters. Often being polite and nonconfrontational when dealing with authorities really freaks them out... it's downright subversive! Better yet, take cops, city managers/councilpersons skating or organize a charity skating event, form a skate patrol... basically do everything you can to break down the "us vs. them" mentality that seems to govern many skater-civilian interactions. Work for more access to skating territory, not less.

Variously-abled funhogs working on accessibility issues...

Speaking of ordinances and liability issues concerning skaters ...if a drunk sanitation worker runs over you with a large garbage truck while you're sitting on a park bench minding your own business, by all means sue the hell out of those responsible! However, if you get hurt in the course of skating by your own actions, **PLEASE REFRAIN FROM SUING ANYBODY:** property owners, city governments, skate & skate component manufacturers, etc.! Accept **responsibility** for the risks you have chosen to take by your own actions, namely **skating!** Inline skating (like skiing, mtn. biking, rugby, river rafting, hang gliding, bungee jumping, kayaking, surfing, rock climbing, automobile driving, alpine mountaineering, etc) is an **inherently dangerous** activity: yo<u>u</u> are responsible for the consequences of your behavior!

175

There are lots of highly-talented "body geniuses" out there who can master advanced skating skills quickly & easily. For the rest of us "body subgeniuses" (whose aerial 360° spins devolve into 180° butt-slams) these things take time and work. Fortunately, it's fun "work" and once you learn some basic skills, it's only a matter of spending lots of time on skates, building an "experience foundation"... talent will surely follow! Remember, there is no absolute right or wrong way to skate or to learn to skate... it's all experimental and you're your own lab rat! Get some ski poles and try some skiing moves, design a birdman suit and fly off big drops, skate naked! One of the coolest things about in-line skating is that you can never fully master it... you're always learning! In essence we are all permanent zen student "grasshoppers", waiting for the master (gravity) to whack us upside the head with a big stick so's we can attain in-line skating enlightenment and ultimately, blading nirvana. It's not the goal, it's the journey! Skate on!

Skating Alpine-style!

Achieve Flight With A Birdman Suit!

Think of Nietzsche's ode to funhogs...
"The secret of reaping the greatest fruitfulness and the greatest enjoyment from life is to live dangerously."

Glossary

Skatespeak-A Glossary
Of Inline Skating Terms

abductors - muscle/tendon group that spreads your legs out. You can do the most basic swizzle with abductors (outstroke) and adductors (instroke). [See "adductor"] alone. If you combine abduction (outstroke) + external rotation (out-torque) plus adduction (in-stroke) + internal rotation (in-torque) you get the far more dynamic and powerfully propulsive "advanced swizzle"! Abductor-adductor motion is also very effective in creating wheel edge friction to bleed speed or govern velocity!

Abduction

"External Rotation": "knee swing out", "outside leg torque"

↑ "out-torque" ↑

Advanced Swizzle: combination of abductor (outstroke) and external rotation (out-torque) [shaded area]

"passive" body

"active" body

active - ① "active body" - intentional body movement to amplify a move or stunt, or...
② "active brake" - a cuff-heel brake mechanism that pushes your brakepad onto the pavement without your having to lift your front three wheels to bring the brake-pad down (as in a "fixed heel brake").

178

adductors- muscle/tendon group that pulls your legs together (simple "instroke"). When used in concert with "internal (leg) rotation" you can do a powerful instroke for swizzling or sculling (see "abductors"). Adduction + internal rotation is the instroke segment of the Advanced Swizzle (shaded areas).

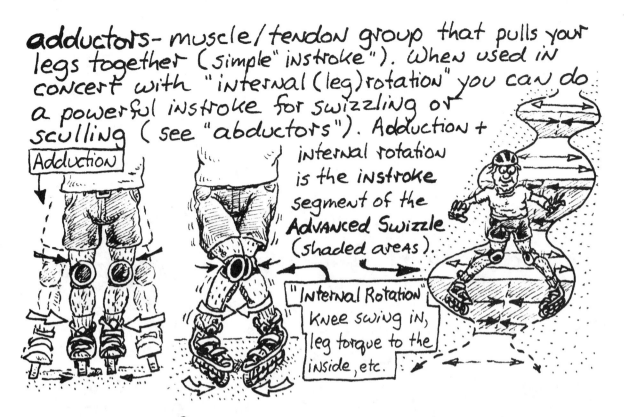

Adduction

"Internal Rotation"
knee swing in,
leg torque to the inside, etc.

aggressive - ① active and committed body movement style: proactive vs. reactive. ② Very daring and enthusiastic street skater. See: "Big Cahone's/Ovaries," "postal". ③ Competition involving grinds, ramps, etc.

airbrakes - an upright and open (untucked) stance that creates excessive wind drag, or baggy clothing also causing wind drag or both. Wind drag is the bane of racerheads, thus the lycra outfits and radical tucks. See "antilycra".

A-Line - A very stable & high control beginner posture wherein knees are close together with the skates out, shoulder-wide or wider. A-Lining tilts your skates onto the inside edges, creating a big footprint* for maximum grip and friction speed control. Variations: "stance", "shuffle", "turn", etc.

* square inches of rubber on the ground

amp (amped) - amplified body movement used to max out a move or trick. Also a particularly aggressive approach to overall style. See "dynamic".

antilycra - baggy/oversize hip-hop style skating attire favored by urban street skaters. Functional too; it's an **airbrake** and soft **body armor**! See "lycra".

antirocker - a wheel configuration used by grinders/railsliders to maximize contact with the rail (or edge) and the frame of the boot. Done by axle realignment

grind plate

or by using small wheels in the center positions (#2 and #3). Additional "grind plates" can be mounted to reduce abrasion on the actual frame. See "rocker."

arc - a curving vector or portion of a spin circle.

backside - to do a trick and/or dismount **back** first.

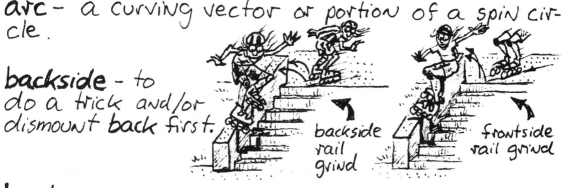

backside rail grind

frontside rail grind

bad - good.

badge - unarmed security guard.

bailout - to take intentional action to remove yourself from a potentially dangerous & deteriorating situation such as a **runaway**. See "grassdive".

bash - to skate down stairs, striking each tread as you go down. See "stair ride".

baseball slide - semi-controlled, laidout, sliding fall. Usually hands-first @, or feet-first ⓑ.

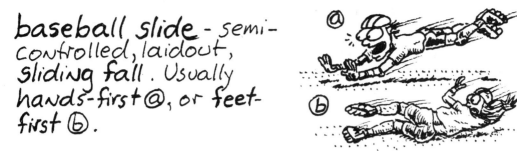

beaucoup-("boo-coo") a shitload, lots of...

beginner - (a.k.a.-"car bait","bozo","geek," etc.) inexperienced skater, first time skater, a civilian on wheels. See -"Novice".

biff- to fall **hard** onto concrete or to T-bone an immovable object; **the** sound your body makes when you slam into the planet & air is forced out of your lungs.

big cahone's - bold male skater, **bad boy**.

big ovaries - bold woman skater, **bad grrl**.

black ice - smooth fresh black asphalt paving or patching. Literally "black ice" when **wet!**

blue hair - elderly female driver of a big "boat car." Usually all you see is knuckles clutching the wheel and a tuft of blue hair.

ohmygod!

body check-(hockey term) to body-slam a civilian, other skater or large objects (trees, taxis, bushes, etc). An excellent way to cause a **runaway beginner** to execute a **grassdive** or bailout in a dangerous situation. See "T-Bone", "grassdive".

body english - any **active** body movement or **torque** to amp a move or steer dynamically. See "carve", "surf."

bomb - to go as fast as possible at the very edge of control...skating Nirvana! See "jammin'"

brainbucket - (a.k.a. "helmet", "skid lid", etc.) Cranium protection device to prevent NON-chemical related brain damage. Helmets work best when actually worn!

No brain, No pain!

bust-a-move - to do a stunt or tricky move. Archaic term.

see "Shortdog"

mad Dog

butt armor - hockey girdle or padded skating shorts.

butt fall - Taking a hard, NON-sliding fall landing ass first. A frequent event for beginning skaters. (See "butt armor")

butt floss - thong bikini (see "sunrise")

car snot - crankcase drippings in puddles frequently encountered in parking lots, parking structures, etc. See "biff", "buttfall"

cartwheel - vertical body spin, usually intentional. Also to use one's arms to vault over the hood of an automobile. See "bluehair"

carve - a dynamic style or move combining deep leaning, "hard edge" use with velocity and centrifugal force. See "surfin'", "hard edge"

chunk - to knock a chunk out of a wheel stuntin' or doing a grind.

civilian- any NON-skater. (a.k.a.- "duh", "suit" "geek", "biped", "organic obstacle", etc.)

cut-stroke ("cut-turn")- skating backwards this is a ①slashing outside stroke on inside edges that causes a ②turn away from the outstroke. ➡

cutoff angle- When crossover turning, it's the placement of the stepover skate on the inside of the turning arc to tighten the turn. The deeper the stepover, the wider the cutoff angle and the tighter the turn.

cutoff angle →

turning arc

Stepover

decision horizon- the last moment of opportunity to make a move to stop, evade, or turn to avoid an obstacle or execute a a move. Consider your front wheels the "event horizon" and the distance to the decision horizon your reaction time.

shit!

① ② TURN!

event horizon
decision horizon
actual horizon

③ begin turn

dope-"cool", "excellent!"

dedicated- a hardcore skater: serious skater.

duckwalk- beginning forward stroking technique wherein the stroking skates begin and end short outstrokes with the toes of the skates staying angled out.

dude - guy (fem. "dudette") (a.k.a. "bro", "homes").

duh - civilian or particularly clueless skater.

durometer - wheel hardness code : "soft" to "hard"
soft (68a) ← average (74a - 78a) → hard (80a +)

dynamic - (amped, dyno) any ultra-energetic move, series of moves, or stunt.

edge - even though most skate wheels have a rounded profile, when tilted a functional edge is created. Tilting your wheels on edge creates friction, making the turn occur. The more tilt and weight (pressure) you put on the skate the "harder" the edge becomes, making your turn more dynamic. Wheel edge friction is drag created by the increase of the wheels' footprint caused by tilting wheels on outside / inside edges.

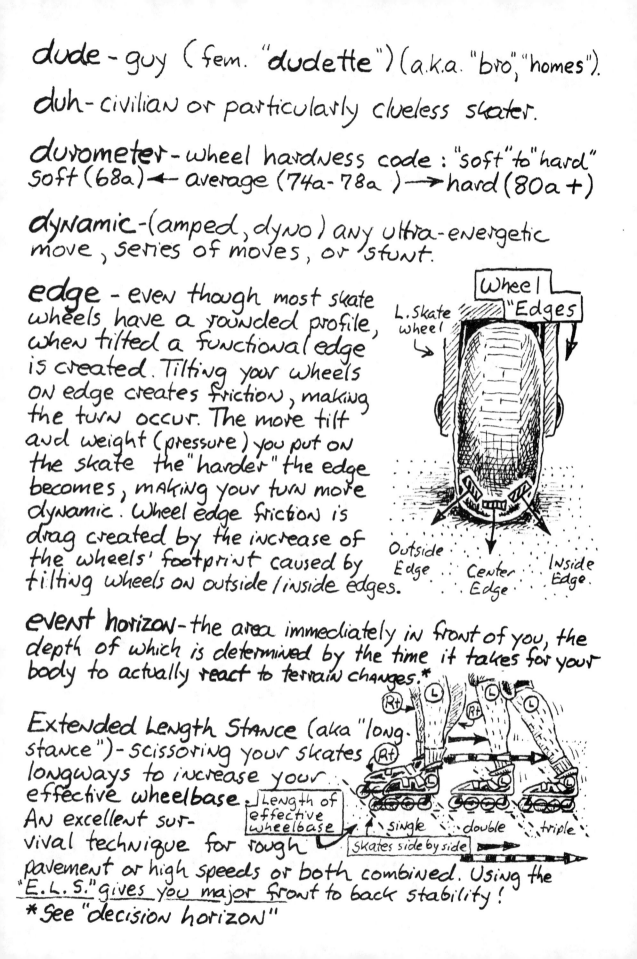

Wheel "Edges"

L. Skate wheel

Outside Edge · · · Center Edge · · · Inside Edge

event horizon - the area immediately in front of you, the depth of which is determined by the time it takes for your body to actually react to terrain changes.*

Extended Length Stance (aka "long stance") - scissoring your skates longways to increase your effective wheelbase. An excellent survival technique for rough pavement or high speeds or both combined. Using the "E.L.S." gives you major front to back stability!

Length of effective wheelbase

single   double   triple

Skates side by side

*See "decision horizon"

extreme ("X-treme", "radical" [archaic]) - the edge of the envelope, very dangerous, etc. "Extreme" is extremely hyped.

face grind - ("full facial," "lip brakes") face fall resulting in a bad case of "**road acne**".

fall line - shortest, steepest route down an incline.

five-0 ("five-oh", "five") - police and any armed security goons.

five wheeler - racing skate (typically) with one extra wheel up front. Faster, more stable, and less maneuverable than regular four-wheel skates. See "racerhead".

Fixed Heel Brake ("F.H.B.", "heel brake")
Non-moving brake apparatus bolted on behind one rear wheel. You engage the brake pad by raising your front three wheels. Very hairy at high speeds! See "active brake".

lift toe → ① engages brake ②

four wheeler ("quads," "trads") old fashioned corner-wheeled skates.

Frankenstein Walk - Beginning level parallel forward "stroking" wherein the skater keeps his/her body quiet and outstrokes by rocking from one foot to the other.

funhog - ("T-type") Person who is involved with any or all of the following "adrenaline sports": skiing, kayaking, mtn. biking, climbing, blading, para-sports, etc. Funhogs are typically adrenaline/dopamine crazed individuals with anarcho-vulgarian tendencies.

185

geezer (a.k.a. "gork", "gomer") male "bluehair."

get air – to temporarily skate off the planet. Zero" to 6"–"baby air", 18" to 36"–"big air", 6' to 12'– "hospital" or "sick"air. See "postal", "gravity god".

glide – riding the roll; second half of a proper forward stride. To roll without adding muscle power.

grassdive – to bail out intentionally onto grass or other soft organic substance (dirt, mulch, etc.).

grassride (a.k.a. "off-roadin'")–to attempt to skate onto grass (as in a bailout) or to practice skating moves on grass where it's safe to fall.

gravity god (s)* – The gravity god giveth and the gravity god taketh away...what goes up, must come down, etc. Skating involves a complex interplay between gravitational forces, velocity, friction and centrifugal force. The wise skater tries to work <u>with</u> gravity, thus avoiding angering the gravity god and having to sacrifice a pound of flesh (literally!) in the form of **holy road rash.**

grind – to slide sideways on curbs, edges, and railing using your frames and soles instead of wheel rolling action. Grinding handrails, guard rails, etc. is usually called railsliding or railriding.

simple frontside curb grind

simple antirocker

grind plate and tiny wheels, unrockered

* Schism: some propose a good "up god" and a bad "down god"

hard edge - to carve a turn, smear, or slide on an inside or outside edge while adding weight (pressure) and pushing to the outside of your arc.

Diagram: rt. foot- hard inside edge. Left foot- hard outside edge → left turn

hard edge

hospital air (a.k.a. "sick air") To execute a vert move or jump that attains a height sufficient to badly injure the skater if the move is blown. Also generic term for "big air."

The Consequences of "Hospital Air"...

in line - ("mono ski") to glide/cruise with your wheels "literally" in line": toe to heel or heel to heel. Skating with your wheels in line requires a good scissor which makes for a very stable stance. To skate in line gives the effect of skiing on a single ski, hence the term "mono (one) ski."

Carving a turn with wheels in line heel to heel

mono ski stance

instroke - when swizzling or sculling, to bring your outstroking skate back to mid-line with a pulling* motion using your inside edges on the instroking skate.

See "adductor"

Sculling Instroke

187

jammin' (a.k.a. "bombing", "screaming") to skate very fast and aggressivly, at the edge of control.

jump - to get air by leaping upward or by going off a drop, ramp, or pipe.

knee brake (a.k.a. "knee slide") to drop to the ground on one or both knees using your knee pads as brake pads (or simply to do a flashy knee pad "slide" move).

knee brake

Knee Slide (or "Fred Astaire") Note - this requires heavy-duty knee pads !!

knee swing - to steer your skates by moving your knees right to left in concert. The "swing" puts both your skates on appropriate "turning edges". Similar to downhill skiing's parallel slalom style.

"knee swings"

laid out (aka "layout") - to go into a horizonal pose after coming off a ramp, pipe, or jump.

laid out

Linda Blair - the technique of twisting your neck and body so as to look behind you in the "blind spot" without losing your balance

The Linda Blair

longstance (See "Extended Length Stance")

lycra - colorful tight-fitting costumery favored by

188

racerheads, speed skaters, etc. to theoretically reduce "wind drag". See "anti lycra", "racerhead"

mono ski (see "in line") Using two 4 wheel skates
to make an 8 wheeled virtual ski.

mush - to skate with a dog or dogs, hopefully
with the dog(s) towing you.

opposite direction foot (aka "O.D.F.") - weighting or
stroking with, for example, a right foot to turn left
or visa versa.

parallel technique - to skate with your feet parallel except when stroking (toes angled out) or turning (toes in, crossover turn)

phat - good, excellent (syn. "dope")

pipe - a concavely curved ramp.

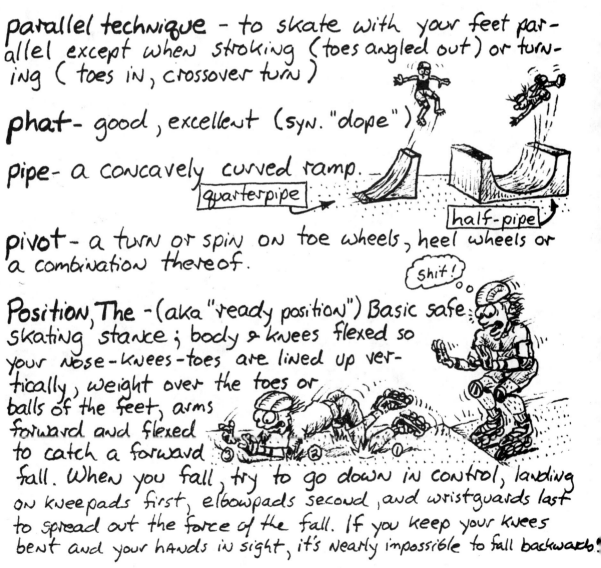

quarterpipe

half-pipe

pivot - a turn or spin on toe wheels, heel wheels or
a combination thereof.

shit!

Position, The - (aka "ready position") Basic safe
skating stance; body & knees flexed so
your nose-knees-toes are lined up ver-
tically, weight over the toes or
balls of the feet, arms
forward and flexed
to catch a forward
fall. When you fall, try to go down in control, landing
on kneepads first, elbowpads second, and wristguards last
to spread out the force of the fall. If you keep your knees
bent and your hands in sight, it's nearly impossible to fall backwards.

posse (aka "krew") skating buds, cohorts.

postal - sanity challenged, wack, kook, u.f.o, etc.

powerslide - advanced stopping method requiring a 90° body turn and skid with your lead skate, perpendicular to your original vector. See "T-stop".

basic powerslide

psychogenic percentagenisis (pron: si-cō-gin-ik per-cent-ā-gin-a-cis) the tendency of arbitrarily designating quantitative values expressed as percentages. Example: ..."80% of skaters like dangerous activities!" According to Dr. H. Wallace*, I'm an egregious example of this brain disorder, although I argue that "PGP" affects nearly 64% of the male population in the western hemisphere.

racerhead - highly competitive skater, the antithesis of the funhog skater ("cruiser"). See "lycra", "antilycra".

railslide (a.k.a. "railride") to grind stair rails, guard rails, etc. see "grind", "Antirocker", "postal"

ramp - any wedge-shaped incline used for jumps and stunts. A concave ramp is a "pipe". See "get air", "hospital air", etc.

Yi !

road rash (aka "road burn", "ramp rash") - friction burns and abrasions caused by a sliding, skidding fall. A small patch of road rash is usually called a "raspberry".

rocker - to offset your wheels in the frames to get a convex wheel configuration. See illustrations, next page.

*original term coined by Dr. H. Wallace, circa 1993

rocker ♪
easy turns, spins

anti-rocker ♪
grinding

unrockered
"normal" skating

Aiiieee

runaway - to lose control of one's velocity on a hill. See "bailout," "roadrash".

runout - flat or uphill stretch at the bottom of a hill for gradual deceleration w/o hazards. A **bad** runout would be a busy intersection.

safety weenie - an extremely conservative skater who tends to wear excessive body armor. See "wüss".

scissor - to extend your stance front to back.

scull (sculling) - half a swizzle. To propel yourself forward by one-footed in/out strokes.

shortdog - handy pocket-size half-pint bottle containing bad wine or spirits.

shuffle - beginner stroking (A-Line or parallel) wherein your body & leg movement is minimized & propulsion is done with little outstrokes by shifting your weight from one foot to the other. See "Frankenstein Walk"

skater - (aka "blader") one who skates.

skitch - to hitch rides surreptitiously by hanging onto back bumpers of cars, trucks, etc. Extremely risky!!

smear - to torque or pivot your wheel edges against

...your vector. The wheels pivot and slide sideways around the pivot point.

Attempting a smear at speed on a rough surface on soft durometer wheels can create the dreaded "velcro effect", sending you flying. See "baseball slide", "road rash", etc.

toe pivot, heel smear

center-weighted circular pivot

speed bleed - related to smearing, this is using **wheel edge friction** and **body torque** to create big friction to **slow** yourself down or **govern** your overall velocity ("speed governor"). You can also bleed speed by using an airscoop stance and/or wearing baggy clothing ("antilycra").

spin - a tight turn (> 45°) done in place or within your vector, done on the ground or in the air. Ground spins are usually done on toe wheels or a toe and heel wheel combination (easiest). A "grounded spin" done with all 8 wheels on the ground is a "**flat spin**"; a slow, stable spin method that's ideal for beginners to get a feel for spin physics. An "air spin" qualifies as a true stunt so don the requisite body armor!

toe spin

flat spin

stair ride (a.k.a. "bash", "stair surf")- to skate down stairs (usually) hitting each tread as you go down. Caution: make sure the treads are wider than your skate is long until you've mastered the trick. Many bashers prefer descending backwards. I prefer sliding the handrail on my butt or stomach (a.k.a. "wuss stairride")

"safe" tread width

192

stall - a static grind move. "frontside" stall, "backside" dismount. Stalling is the first step to learning grinds, slides, & other modes of vertical craziness. ① select an edge 12"-24" off the ground, ② jump onto the edge, hitting between wheels #2 & #3. Hesitate... ③ dismount & don't forget to bend those knees!! When learning stalls, precision counts! (see "buttfall", "biff")

stealth skating - to covertly and unobtrusively skate in semi-legal, ill-egal, or virgin territory (legal but difficult to access). Stealth skating can be done via style (faux walking), dis-guise (huge bellbottoms hid-ing skates) or sneaky be-havior. Getting caught is uncool and fairly **unac-ceptable** since your extra-legal behavior may result in loss of access to skating territory. See "badge", "5-0".

Nightvision goggles make Nocturnal skate adventurism a breeze!

Scissor

stepover - to "step over" an ob-stacle while moving. ① scissor a skate forward, ② step over the obstacle, then ③ repeat on other side. Fast stepovers take superb timing!

street (skating) - semi-aggressive recreational skating in urban/suburban settings. Given the many variables and complexity of the urban skating environment, "street" style skating requires a host of survival skills and beaucoup nerves (see "big cahonés/ovaries")! Also a form of formal competition involving ramps, grinds, railslides, etc. See "aggressive".

stride 'n glide (aka "strokin'") Parallel forward stroking with distinct glide intervals between outstrokes. A good stride 'n glide is stylized, smooth, and very functional (efficient). Adv. intermediate to expert

strollerskate - to push a baby stroller while skating. It's a great way to discharge parental duties while having too much fun! Since stroller-skating moms & dads look so darn cute to everybody (including cops!), you may want to borrow a friend's baby (if you're not a breeder) or acquire a doll and real stroller for some flagrant stealth skating. **Access** is virtually guaranteed!

yeek!

Strollerskate Stuntin'

Stunt - a trick or complex move sequence.

sunrise - what you see looking up a skirt (in a bar, usually)

sunset - the darkness accompanying being **punched** out by the skirt-wearee and/or her significant other for your sunrise **gazing**! Another Dr. H. Wallace term.

Superman slide - laid out hands-first, high-speed sliding wipeout. Hope you were wearin' your heavy-duty wristguards! See "baseball slide", "face grind".

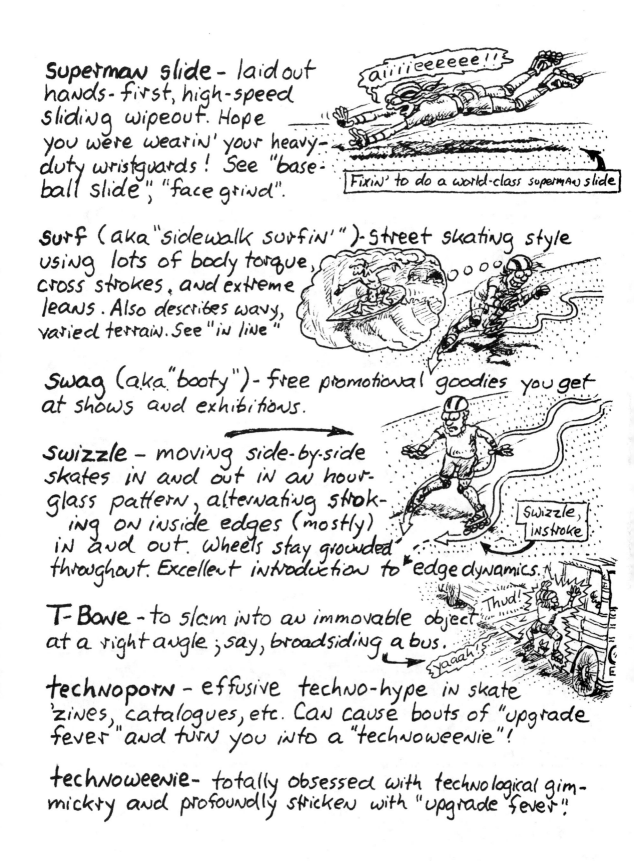

ai!!!eeeeee!!

Fixin' to do a world-class superman slide

surf (aka "sidewalk surfin'") - street skating style using lots of body torque, cross strokes, and extreme leans. Also describes wavy, varied terrain. See "in line"

0000

swag (aka "booty") - free promotional goodies you get at shows and exhibitions.

swizzle - moving side-by-side skates in and out in an hour-glass pattern, alternating strok-ing on inside edges (mostly) in and out. Wheels stay grounded throughout. Excellent introduction to edge dynamics.

Swizzle, instroke

T-Bone - to slam into an immovable object at a right angle; say, broadsiding a bus.

Thud!

yaaah!

technoporn - effusive techno-hype in skate 'zines, catalogues, etc. Can cause bouts of "upgrade fever" and turn you into a "technoweenie"!

technoweenie - totally obsessed with technological gim-mickry and profoundly stricken with "upgrade fever"!

195

thong - (a.k.a. "beach armor") See "buttfloss"

thrash (-ing) - ① very aggressive pavement surfing, ② unnecessary flailing body movement.

tilt - skate angle from side to side. The result of ① leaning the leg/body or from ② ankle tilt, foot twist

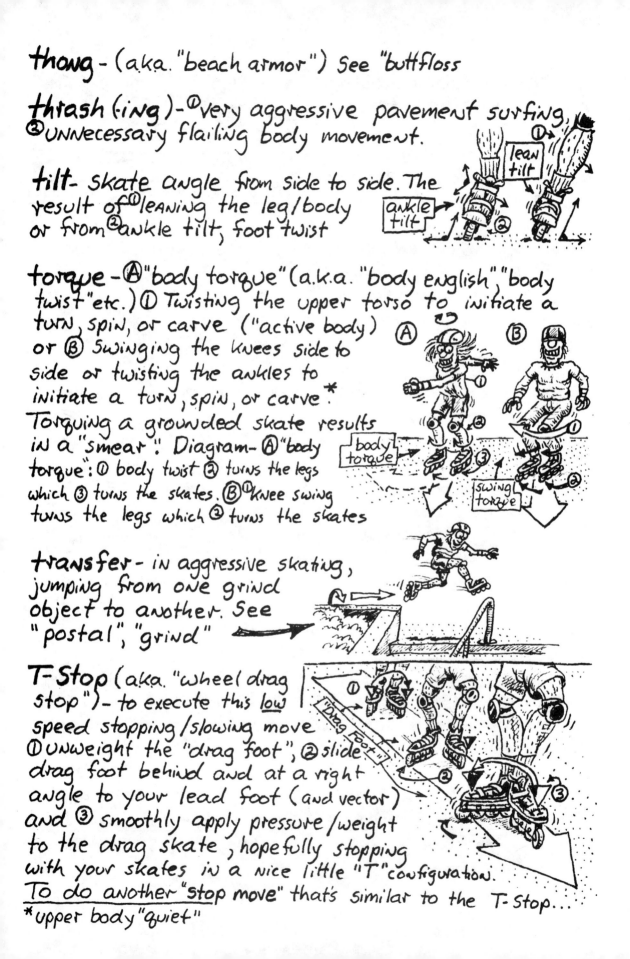

torque - Ⓐ "body torque" (a.k.a. "body english", "body twist" etc.) ① Twisting the upper torso to initiate a turn, spin, or carve ("active body) or Ⓑ swinging the knees side to side or twisting the ankles to initiate a turn, spin, or carve.* Torquing a grounded skate results in a "smear". Diagram- Ⓐ "body torque": ① body twist ② turns the legs which ③ turns the skates. Ⓑ ① knee swing turns the legs which ② turns the skates

transfer - in aggressive skating, jumping from one grind object to another. See "postal", "grind"

T-Stop (a.k.a. "wheel drag stop") - to execute this <u>low</u> speed stopping/slowing move ① unweight the "drag foot", ② slide drag foot behind and at a right angle to your lead foot (and vector) and ③ smoothly apply pressure/weight to the drag skate, hopefully stopping with your skates in a nice little "T" configuration.
<u>To do another "stop move"</u> that's similar to the T-Stop...
*upper body "quiet"

① Unweight and raise the heel of your "inside" skate, drag the toe wheel which ② toe pivots your skate 180° and turns your body 90° to your vector. Smear your "outside" skate (Ⓛ) to slow yourself sufficiently to stop at 90° in the "T-stop position", ③.

speed bleed. smear

pivot

Spinning T-Stop

tuck - to pull your body in to create minimum wind drag to go fast or to prolong a glide. See "airbrake", "lycra", "antilycra".

tucked glide

untucked

turn - ① to change direction on a curving vector (Ⓐ) or ② to change direction at an angle to your vector (Ⓑ). Spins occur within your vector or can be used to create new vectors off 360°!

parallel turn

toe pivot turn Ⓑ

tweaked (aka "tricked out", "honed", "tarted up") - to polish tricks, moves, etc. or to upgrade/fine-tune skates or components to maximize performance. See "upgrade".

über wüss - <u>ve</u>ry conservative, stunt-wise.*

understroke - a stroke crossing under your body on an "outside" edge (usually). The "underskate" is used as the outside skate enabling the ①stepover during the "crossover turn". The ②understroke can be used without the stepover on a turn to bleed speed by creating <u>major wheel edge friction</u>.

*For example, me !

197

upgrade - to retrofit or otherwise technically improve your skates or components thereof. "Upgrade Fever" - the result of reading too much "technoporn." Untreated, this condition can result in permanent "technoweenieism."

vector - in physics, vectors are straight lines of momentum. <u>My</u> cartoon vectors, however, curve and loop all over the place.

slalom vector

velcroed - to experience sudden "wheel stick" resulting in a wipeout because your wheels decided to grip hard*. Example: hockey stop on concrete on 68a "softie" wheels.

shiiitt!

Thud!

Getting velcroed

vert - spectacular moves in competition (or just stuntin' around) in a pipe (¼ or ½).

wallride - to leap upward and "skate" on a vertical plane, a wall for instance.

HUH?

wax - ① to defeat/disable an opponent, or ② to apply wax on surfaces you're gonna grind to speed things up and lessen frame abrasion.

weighting - how you distribute your ① body weight to each skate for different performance characteristics; or ② how you apply pressure/weight inside your boot to micro-adjust boot/skate tilt side to side or front to back (example - <u>toeweighting</u> to do a toe pivot)

Ⓐ Shift
Ⓑ lift
② pivot Ⓒ

① unweighting a foot

*unexpectedly

198

wired - to have a move or stunt fully committed to body memory from much practice (see "tweaked). Also, what happens when you ingest too many triple latte's!

woofed - to go down suddenly without warning, as in falling into an open manhole or getting your wheels stuck in a drain grate while jammin'.

wristguard (a.k.a. "wrist brace") - after your helmet, the most important piece of safety gear you can wear to prevent unnecessary skating injuries!! In 85%* of falls, you will smack the pavement on your hands first! I recommend heavy-duty glove style wristguards for most skating environments.

Besides, if you bust your wrist wearing wristguards, you'll make the paramedics very happy!

E.M.S. Metropolitan 911

E.M.T. "Humor"

har har!

Yo Fred! Just grab th' stretcher. These skaters come PRESPLINTED!

Arrrrgggh...

wüss (a.k.a. "wimp", "punk", "pussy", etc.) derogatory term for timid or hyper-conservative skaters.

"X"/Extreme - way out there. Way dangerous. The usual hype.

*good example of my psychogenic percentagenisis affliction.

Author/Illustrator William "Not-Bill" Nealy
lives in the woods outside Chapel Hill, North
Carolina with his editor and permanent girlfriend
Holland "Dr. H." Wallace and an assortment of
dogs, lizards, pigs, snakes, turtles and amphi-
bians. This is his tenth book.